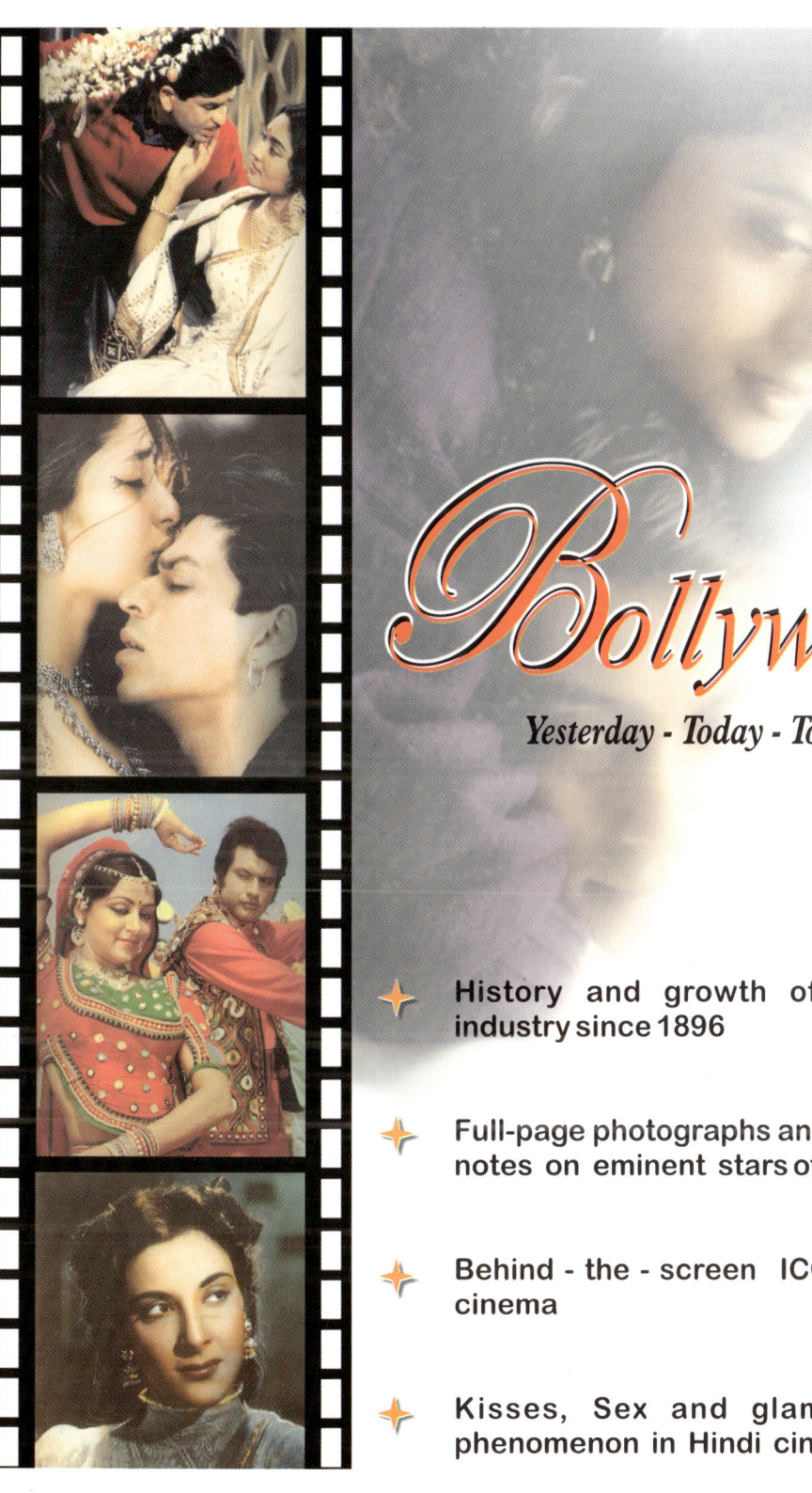

Bollywood
Yesterday - Today - Tomorrow

✦ History and growth of Indian film industry since 1896

✦ Full-page photographs and biographical notes on eminent stars of Hindi cinema

✦ Behind - the - screen ICONS of Indian cinema

✦ Kisses, Sex and glamour, a new phenomenon in Hindi cinema.

*This book is dedicated to
all those film personalities who were
honoured with*
**LIFE-TIME ACHIEVEMENT
AWARDS**
*for their contributions in various fields,
and bringing Indian film industry
on the top of world map!*

Ramesh Dawar

Yesterday-Today-Tomorrow

©Publishers 2006

ISBN-1-905863-01-2
9781905863013

Rights of publication of this book in any language or in any format are the sole property of the publishers, and no part of contents, including artwork, of this book can be produced in any form, without the written consent of the publishers.

Acknowledgment

The Author and the Publishers gratefully acknowledge the cooperation from various sources which provided parts of the material, and also the pictures, included in this book.

Our thanks are also due to Ms Manju Gupta who helped in editing and revising the material of the book.

Published by Star Publications Pvt. Ltd., New Delhi -110 002
for/ on behalf of

INDIAN BOOK SHELF,
55, Warren Street, LONDON W1T 5NW (U.K.)
(E-mail: indbooks@aol.com)

First edition: 2006

Cover designing, artwork and typesetting by:
K[akriti Production, New Delhi-110066

Printing and processing:
Everest Press, New Delhi -110020

INDEX

Indian cinema, history and growth since 1895 7
Kissing, sex and glamour, a new phenomenon 12
Twinkling stars of Hindi cinema (in alphabetical order):

Ashok Kumar	15
Amitabh Bachchan	18
Aamir Khan	21
Abhishek Bachchan	24
Aishwarya Rai	26
Ajay Devgan	29
Anil Kapoor	32
Dev Anand	34
Dharmendra	37
Dilip Kumar	40
Esha Deol	43
Guru Dutt	45
Hema Malini	48
Hrithik Roshan	51
Jaya Bachchan	54
John Abraham	57
Juhi Chawla	59
Kajol	61
Kareena Kapoor	63
Karishma Kapoor	66
K.L. Saihgal	68
Lata Mangeshkar	71
Madhubala	74
Madhuri Dixit	77
Meena Kumari	80
Nargis	83
Nutan	86
Pran	88

Preity Zinta	91
Prem Chopra	94
PrithviRaj Kapoor	96
Raj Kapoor	99
Rani Mukherjee	103
Rekha	106
Saif Ali Khan	108
Salman Khan	110
Sanjay Dutt	113
Sanjeev Kumar	116
Shabana Azmi	119
Shammi Kapoor	121
Shah Rukh Khan	124
Shashi Kapoor	128
Sunny Deol	131
Sunil Dutt	134
Sushmita Sen	137
Vyjyanthimala	140
Waheeda Rehman	142

* * *

History and growth of Indian cinema

The birth of the cinema took place when the world's first film by Lumiere brothers was screened at Grand Café in Indian Room Hall, Paris on 28 December 1895 in the presence of about thirty-five persons. Subsequently in the year 1896 the film made by George Melies was screened after a gap of about six months. The screening of Lumiere brothers' films took place on 7 July 1896 in India. The first cinema show was held in a room at Watson's Hotel that later came to be known as Esplanade Mansion in Bombay. The Indian viewer took the new experience as something already familiar to him. Only 200 persons attended the show after paying two rupees each. The films screened were 'Entry of Cinematograph', 'Arrival of a Train', 'The Sea Bath' 'A Demolition', 'Workers Leaving the Factory', 'Ladies and Soldiers on Wheels', etc. There were four shows from 6 p.m. onward. The audience were held spellbound. They were thrilled when they saw a train coming upon them on the screen. The visual effect of these ten-minute duration films was great. There were two shows a day of twelve short films. Fortunately, the still photographer Harishchandra Sakharam Bhatwadekar was also one of the spectators in the show and was known as Saave Dada. Dada was keen on getting hold of the Lumiere cinematograph and trying it out himself rather than show the Lumiere films to a wider audience. The public reception accorded to Wrangler Paranjpaye at Chowpatty on his return from England with the coveted distinction he got at Cambridge was covered by Bhatwadekar in December 1901 and the first Indian topical or actuality film was born.

In 1898, Bhatwadekar began shooting a wrestling match held in Bombay's Hanging Gardens. He produced his second film on training of circus monkeys and sent it to England for development. He also filmed the coronation ceremony of Edward VII in India in 1903. Signor Colonello and Cornaglia (Italians) screened films successfully during 1897 and 1898 in Bombay. During 1899 a British cameraman shot Indian events like 'Our Indian Regime', 'Great Imambada of Lucknow' and 'Arrival of a Train' at Bombay Railway Station. Other enthusiasts like P.B. Mehta opened his cinema America-India and J.N. Tata installed a cinema apparatus for private screening of films at different centres of Bombay.

In Calcutta, Hiralal Sen photographed scenes from some of the plays at the Classic Theatre. Such films were shown as added attractions after the stage performances were taken to distant venues, where the stage performers could not reach. The possibility of reaching a large audience through recorded images projected several times through mechanical gadgets caught the fancy of people in the performing arts and the stage and entertainment business. The first decade of the 20th century saw live and recorded performances being clubbed together in the same programme. J.F. Madan started the film business in 1902 in a tent called 'Bioscope' at Calcutta and he enriched his business enormously by 1907. He was the first man to establish the permanent theatre called Elphinstone Picture Palace at Calcutta in 1907 and was the man behind the first feature film to come out from Bengal 'Nal Damayanti' in 1921 in which leading roles were played by Patience Cooper, K. Adjania and Italian film stars. The strong influence of its traditional arts, music, dance and popular theatre on the cinema movement in India in its early days is probably responsible for the characteristic enthusiasm for inserting song and dance sequences in Indian films which continues till today.

Regular screening of films was started by M.D. Sethna in his touring cinema company in 1904 at Bombay. Mr Pathe also thought it better to start screening of films regularly in 1907 to boost the patronage of cinema-loving people. Pathe Cinema India (Bombay) specialised in educational films and in industrial, travel, scientific, animal studies, growth of plants, deep-sea inhabitant and bird life, etc. This gave impetus to many others to start screening of such films in different parts of the country. Since it was the silent era, films originating from anywhere could be seen in India. By this time still photography had been developed as an established business as well as art in India. By and large the English film shows were held in cinema halls by the end of 1910 in major centres of the country.

Dhundiraj Govind Phalke (1860-1944), affectionately called Dadasaheb Phalke, a multifaceted and versatile personality was born on 30 April 1870 at Trambkeshwar in Nasik in a Brahmin family. At the age of fourty four the first time he saw a movie named 'Life of Christ' in a tent cinema in 1910 during Christmas at Bombay. He was strongly taken in by the film. He could not sleep the whole night. Next day he saw the film with his wife and thought as to how to make such films on the topics of early life of Lord Krishna, Kalia Mardan, Kans Vadh, etc. He read lots of literature, books and journals on filmmaking and successfully experimented his knowledge by making a film *'The Birth of a Pea Plant'* in a pot. This encouraged him to go to London on 1 February 1912 to purchase a movie camera. The editor of magazine Bioscope, Mr Kayborn, helped him in purchasing the machine and apparatus from London. He also got him trained in different sections of filmmaking. Ultimately, Dada Phalke reached Bombay on 1 April 1912 with a Williamson camera, other film development apparatus, raw films, etc.

Phalke fixed up a studio in Dadar Main Road, wrote the scenario, erected the sets and started shooting for his first venture *'Raja Harishchandra'* in 1913. The first full-length story of Phalke was completed in 1912 and released at the Coronation Cinema on 1 May 1913, for special invitees and members of the press. The film was widely acclaimed by one and all and proved to be a great success. The film was 3,700 feet long and took seven months and twenty-seven days in the making. The hero of the film was a stage-actor Dabke and the role of Taramati was performed by a man named Salunke while his son acted as Rohtash in the film. The film was a milestone in the history of Indian cinema. The single print of the film proved to be a fortune-spinner, suggesting the commercial viability of films, and providing an index of public response. Phalke is regarded as the father of Indian cinema. Central to his career as a filmmaker was his fervent belief in the nationalistic philosophy of swadeshi, which advocated that Indians should take charge of their own economy in the perspective of future Independence.

A film *'Setu Bandhan'* in Hindi was a synchronised film that came next and was released as a talkie in 1934. His first full-length talkie was a devotional feature film *'Gangavataran'* in Hindi and Marathi and was released in 1937. He was a misfit in talkie cinema and he had grown old by now. He left for his heavenly abode on 16 February 1944 at Nasik and by that time people had forgotten this father of Indian cinema. However, today in 2006, it seems Nasik has woken up after a long gap to its old hero and is celebrating Phalke's birth anniversary for the first time in 136 years down the line. A project is being worked out to keep his memory alive in this temple town.

During these years a number of enthusiasts came forward to experiment and make silent feature films on various themes and subjects. Some of the films produced in those years are landmarks in the history of Indian cinema. In Bengal, a region rich in culture and intellectual activity, the first Bengali feature film in 1917 was a remake of Phalke's *'Raja Harishchandra'*. Titled *'Satyawadi Raja Harishchandra'*, it was directed by Rustomjee Dotiwala. Less prolific than the Bombay-based film industry, around 122 feature films were made in Calcutta in the silent era. The first talkie film *'Melody of Love'* was screened in the country in 1929 at Elphinstone Picture Palace, Calcutta.

In 1926, A.M. Irani formed the Imperial Film Company and produced the film *'Anarkali'* in 1928 with Sulochana and D. Billimoria in the lead roles. It was a legendary film. They produced some other films too.

The first Indian talkie feature film *'Alam Ara'* produced by Imperial Film Company and directed by Ardeshir M. Irani, featuring Master Vithal and Zubeida was released on 14 March 1931 at Majestic Cinema in Bombay. Basically this film was written for Parsi Theatre based on magic drama. The other attractions of this film included its enchanting seven songs, although Irani earlier had produced one silent movie titled *'Veer Abhimanyu'* in 1922.

In 1931, the Tamil film *'Kalidas'* directed by H.M. Reddy was released as also was *'Marthandavarma'* directed by P.V. Rao. The last named got into a legal tangle and was withdrawn after its premiere. Based on a novel by C.V. Raman Pillai, a few of its title credits and action made obvious references to the swadeshi movement of the time. Had it not been for the legal embargo, the film would have had a great impact on the regional cinema of the south.

With the birth of talkie cinema a number of film enterprises flourished in addition to the earlier famous companies like Ranjit Movietone, Wadia Movietone, Bombay Talkies, Prabhat Film Company and New Theatres Limited. Up to Independence, i.e. 1947, the filmmakers produced a number of good and memorable films of social, moral, cultural, historical, action, classical, costume drama, fantasy, devotional, mythological themes and on communal harmony. Only very few filmmakers tactfully incorporated the themes of freedom in their films either in the form of subject, story, scenes, dialogues and song. It was only to escape the eyes and wrath of the British rulers and incite and encourage the Indian masses to participate in the freedom struggle. A striking example of this is the song of the film *'Kismet'* in 1943 — *'Door hato aye duniya walon Hindustan hamara hai…'*

Then came the *'golden fifties'* that saw the rise of great directors like Mehboob Khan, Bimal Roy, Guru Dutt and Raj Kapoor who changed the fate of Indian cinema. These directors entered the film industry during the 1930s and 40s, which were traumatic years for the Indians. The fight for Independence, famines, changing social mores, global fight against fascism contributed to the ethos in which the director grew up.

Mehboob Khan remade his film *'Aurat'* in 1940 in colour and with drastically different imagery as *'Mother India'* in 1957. It was a stupendous success and later even acquired an epic status. The story revolved around Radha, played by Nargis, one of the strongest woman characters of Indian cinema. Her husband having lost both the arms in an accident leaves her alone; she raises her children while fending off financial as well as sexual pressures from the moneylender. Highly successful and critically acclaimed, Mehboob's films depicted the clash between pre-capitalist ruralism and an increasingly modernised state with the commercial-industrial practices and values.

Bimal Roy's directorial debut with 'Udayer Pathey' in 1944 introduced a new era of post-World War romantic-realist melodrama. His 'Do Bigha Zamin' in 1953 and 'Sujata' were two of the most notable films to depict reformism and humanism. 'Do Bigha Zamin' was one of the first Indian films to chart mass migration of rural people to cities and their degradation in urban slums. 'Sujata' dealt with the subject of untouchability.

Guru Dutt entered the Hindi film industry as an actor. His early films were entertainers like 'Aar Paar' in 1954, 'Mr and Mrs 55' in 1955 and 'CID' in 1956. With the darkly romantic 'Pyaasa' in 1957, Dutt launched a cycle of films that have remained India's most spectacular achievements in melodrama. 'Kaagaz ke Phool' in 1959 was the first cinemascope and autobiographical in nature.

Raj Kapoor was a megastar, successful producer and a director. He set up the RK Films in 1948 and made 'Aag', 'Awara', 'Shri 420', 'Bobby' in 1973 and 'Satyam Shivam Sundaram' in 1978 which became huge hits, after which came the commercial failure of his most ambitious project 'Mera Naam Joker' in 1970.

During the last fifty years, in particular, there have been a lot of changes in the trends in Indian cinema. Though the technique and quality of Indian films has tremendously improved, there have been variations in themes and subjects also. There was a time when family issues dominated Bollywood films, then came the films based on crime, followed by an era of films on patriotism like 'Shaheed', 'Upkaar', and then came the films on Indian politics and war like 'Haqeeqat', 'Border', 'LOC', 'Mission Kashmir'. Finally came the time when most of the films were dominated by romance, music, sex and glamour, and the recent trend is of films on terrorism and crime, like 'Fanna'. A few years from hence, maybe a new trend will be seen.

* * *

Kisses, glamour and sex in Hindi cinema

Glamour, sex and kissing scenes on the screen have always been a cause of debate and controversy in India. Youths from different parts of the country would often leave their home to rush to Bombay in the hope of acting as a hero in Hindi films even during the silent era of Indian cinema.

In this early silent era of Indian '*bioscope*', the majority of films were based on mythological, historical or social themes. The filmmakers knew the pulse of the audience, and were aware of how to attract the masses so as to make their films commercially viable. There was not much of a problem during those days on inclusion of glamour, sex or kissing scenes in films. A number of early films showed glamour with kissing scenes shot freely and without any restrictions by the then British government. Producer Soraj F. Company's '*Mukti Sangram*' in 1926, '*Shiraz*' in 1929 (a historical film starring Enakshi Rama Rao and Charu Roy), Imperial Company's '*Heer Ranjha*' with Sulochana and D. Billimoria, '*Himmat-e-Marda*' in 1935 with Lalita Pawar exposing her thigh and with Devika Rani kissing producer-actor Himanshu Rai created a turmoil in those days. Films based on romance were first introduced by none other than Himanshu Rai.

Kissing between two human beings is a natural phenomenon, but most filmmakers depict such a scene for the sake of gaining commercial advantage and publicity by creating a sensation. Exploitation of glamour, sex and kissing on the screen are the major interests of the filmmakers of today. In the early films kissing was shown very subtly as a peck on the cheek of the heroine. But nowadays, lip-to-lip kissing in the Hollywood style seems to have become the order of the day. The Indian Censor Board has also relaxed its rules as to allow provocative, exotic, sizzling, glamorous, sexy and kissing scenes on the screen. Some filmmakers are of the view that it is the demand of the public and without introducing such sensuous scenes in their films, they face the risk of their films bombing at the box-office.

After Independence, the filmmakers turned selective in their choice of the subjects for their films. They kept in mind the fact that their films would be seen not only by individuals but also their families. Keeping in view the Indian culture, they tactfully through different signs and symbols began to shoot love and sex scenes, so that no hue and cry would be raised by social activists. Even the glamour scenes were shot keeping in mind the Indian culture. The major attractions of films during those days were their melodious songs, catchy music, and powerful dialogues with interesting themes. Body exposure was kept to the minimum. The heroines wore full-sleeved blouses with sarees or with long skirts.

Over passage of time, this style of dress has now become obsolete, redundant and is looked upon as a sign of backwardness. The use of the skimpiest of blouses and mini skirts has now become a sign of modern culture. The bathing costume and bikini facilitate a heroine to expose her body liberally and without hesitation. The more she exposes the more contracts she gets. At times, the scenes are so blatantly sensuous that members of a family cannot see such films with either their children or their elders.

Whether required or not, some of the filmmakers incorporate glamorous, sexy or kissing scenes for no rhyme or reason obviously with the objective of targeting the youth and the middle-class cine-goers. At times they shoot very exotic and sizzling item numbers to woo the international market, particularly in conservative nations like the Middle East or South-east Asia. Sex, glamour and fast action have become a fashion today. Filmmakers seem to be competing with each other in depicting glamour to the maximum and manage to get it passed by whatever means available by the Censor Board.

The presentation of glamour and sex in films artistically is acceptable, but who will decide which of the scenes is artistically done? The arguments and counter-arguments may differ from man to man according to place, time and environment. Portrayal of heroines in gorgeous costumes, short skirts, bikinis, swimsuits, provocative dresses on the screen has become a necessary prerequisite for every successful film.

Some intelligent filmmakers in today's era are interested to produce or direct films only on marital relations which provide them ample scope to exhibit semi-nude or sensitive parts of the heroine's body. The reason touted for such blatant exposure is either the need for them or due to their so-called aesthetic value. They even go to the extent of justifying their inclusion by saying that even our ancient heritage and culture depicted the same through Khajuraho and Ajanta or Ellora sculptures. The objective is to make the masses addicted to their films through depiction of obscene or steamy, sexy scenes that are titillating. Such scenes merely succeed to heighten desire instead of adding to the aesthetic values.

Bollywood's greatest showman, the late Raj Kapoor, presented his heroines in the most bewitching, glamorous, voluptuous and exotic postures in his films. His films were successful at the box-office and were patronised by the masses not only in India, but abroad too. In 'Barsaat' in 1949, a most intimate and artistically glamour scene was shot with Nargis falling into Raj Kapoor's arms. Subsequently the scene with the hero holding a violin in one hand and a girl in the other was adopted as the logo for RK Films. The biographical film 'Mera Naam Joker' in 1970 was shot artistically with heroine Padmini clad in only a saree, Simi Garewal exposing her thigh before a young Raju, and K. Ryabinkyna, the Russian actress being kissed by Raju. The film proved a disaster and Raj Kapoor became nearly bankrupt. The story of young lovers in 'Bobby' in 1973 was a super hit with the heroine Dimple Kapadia in this debut film of hers looking bewitching in a swimsuit. Artistically framed the film 'Satyam Shivam Sundaram' in 1978 gave a maximum number of chances to the heroine Zeenat Aman to expose herself in different sizzling and sensual poses. 'Ram Teri Ganga Maili' in 1985 was another film of Raj Kapoor and in this Rajeev Kapoor kissed Mandakini in a most sensual manner. Raj Kapoor was a master at filming a woman's body as also passionate love scenes in an artistic style.

Of late 'Jism' has been the first movie to depict a full kissing scene on the screen between John Abraham and Bipasha Basu. The film 'Murder' is another example of such a scene between Emran Hashmi and Mallika Sherawat. Govind Nihalani's 'Dev' too shows an intimate kiss between Fardeen Khan and Kareena Kapoor. The film 'Asoka' was gorgeous and full of glamorous scenes. In 'Mumbai se Aaya Mera Dost' a kiss scene became the turning point in the film that had Lara Dutta. The film 'Tumsa Nahin Dekha' started with a kiss between Emran Hashmi and Diya Mirza and closed with an intimate kiss scene too between them. Rani Mukherjee and Kareena Kapoor, both kiss Hrithik Roshan on each side of his cheeks at the same time in 'Mujhse Dosti Karoge' in 2002. In 'Sarfarosh' Aamir Khan and Sonali Bendre sizzle in the rain; a long kiss scene is shown in 'Raja Hindustani' between Aamir Khan and Karishma Kapoor; provocative scenes by Sushmita Sen are seen in 'Chingari'; followed by Rehana Sultana's exposure of long legs in 'Chetna'; a long nude shot of Smriti Biswas in 'Bandit Queen' and many of Parveen Babi in different films and who threw all caution to the winds when performing glamorous scenes. Films remained hot during their releases due to intimate kisses, glamour or sexy postures as seen in 'Boom' (a long kissing scene between Jackie Shroff and Madhu Sapre), films 'Oops' and 'Footpath' (in the latter was a kiss between Bipasha Basu and Aftaab Shivdasani), 'Mohabbatein' (a hot kiss between Shamita Shetty and Aaditya Chopra) and the film 'Pyaar Tune Kya Kiya' created a sensation among the youth. Nowadays Mallika Sherawat has become a kissing icon. There were seventeen kisses in the film 'Khawhish'. She herself publicised these scenes. Being called a sex symbol does not embarrass her but her family members in the small town of Rohtak, Haryana, hide their heads in shame. She comfortably gave kissing scenes in the film 'Shaadi se Pehley' in 2006 with Akshay Khanna too. There are a number of films which can be cited for their depiction of glamour, sex and kissing scenes.

When girls first began exposing on the screen, there was much hue and cry. But today it has become absolutely normal to depict such scenes in films. Today's girls treat the exposure scenes very professionally, totally unconcerned about what other people might think. They take it as a normal shot. Morality in Hindi cinema is changing very fast. For argument's sake they ask, what is wrong with kissing on the screen? Don't people kiss in their personal lives? Why is there a hitch in showing a kiss scene on the screen?

Seeing the trends and practices, the present era of Bollywood has become the era of glamour, sex, kiss and action. Glamour plays a huge part in a heroine's career. Sex is not a taboo nowadays. How long and far will this go in India no one can tell, but certainly a day will come when the entire Hollywood culture will prevail upon Indian culture. Then there would be no Censor Board in India to restrict such aping of Western culture in films. And what of Indian culture? Maybe, it will die a slow death giving way to Western culture, but where will the Western culture go then? Will it become more decadent or will it go back to its roots? Let the coming generation ponder over this question.

* * *

Ashok Kumar

Kumud Lal Kunjilal Ganguly alias Ashok Kumar Ganguly was lovingly and respectfully called Dadamoni in Bollywood. He never wanted to be an actor but life took such a turn that he landed in the film industry and became a versatile and successful hero. He was conferred the Dada Saheb Phalke Award on 31 May 1989 and honoured with the Padma Shri by President Dr Rajendra Prasad in 1962. He won the Sangeet Natak Akademi Award in 1959, the Filmfare Awards for '*Raakhi*' in 1962 and for '*Ashirwaad*' in 1969.

Born on 13 October 1911 at Bhagalpur in Bihar at his maternal grandfather's place, he was the son of Kunjilal Ganguly, a prominent advocate of Khandwa and a Bengali Brahmin, and mother Gouri Rani Devi, who was the grand daughter of Raja Shibchandra Banerjee. He was the eldest while his brothers Anup was nearly fifteen years and Kishore twenty years his junior. He also had a younger sister Sati Rani who was married to Sasadhar Mukherjee, a successful film producer. Ashok's father moved to Khandwa, Madhya Pradesh and admitted his sons to school. Soon Ashok shifted to Jabalpur for appearing in the intermediate science examination and later on to Nagpur for completing his graduation in science. He went to Calcutta for studying law but had no interest in becoming an advocate. He wanted to be a film director, so he decided to join films and left for Bombay. When his parents heard about his decision, they were very angry and disappointed. In those days, acting was not considered an honourable profession and actors were looked down upon. They were believed to come from the lowest strata of society.

Ashok Kumar initially joined Bombay Talkies as a technician. He initially worked in the camera department and after a few months became a lab assistant. He learnt all the techniques of filmmaking, with no desire to become an actor. He was neither good-looking nor chocolate-faced like the heroes of that era.

One day a worried Himanshu Rai, founder and chief of Bombay Talkies, came to him to request him to act as the leading man in his film '*Jeevan Naiya*', whose hero Najmul Hassan was missing. Since all arrangements and planning had already been done, Himanshu Rai pleaded with him saying that he would lose a lot of money if Ashok Kumar were not agree to his offer. Ashok, on his part, was most reluctant to become an actor. But after persuasion and for the sake of this film, he agreed to do the film. The debut film was released in 1936 and he also sang the song '*Koi humdum na raha…*' Himanshu Rai advised him not to leave the line. His style of acting was very natural. Ashok agreed and began to take this profession seriously. His salary was only seventy-five rupees per month. His next film '*Achhut Kanya*' became a much talked about film, marking the emergence of social films in India. The film was a big hit. He sang his own song in his voice '*Tu ban ki chidiya, main ban ka panchi, ban ban doloon re…*' which became an instant hit.

While working on his next film, '*Vachan*' in 1938, Ashok got married to the Bhagalpur girl, Shobha, who hailed from Dhanbad. She proved to be a dedicated wife, who died at the time of her fiftieth wedding anniversary. She gave birth to a son, Aroop and three daughters — Bharati, Roopa and Priti. His films like '*Kangan*', '*Bandhan*', '*Izzat*', '*Savitri*' and '*Janambhumi*', etc. earned him fame by

1940. The films fared well and were great hits; his career had now taken off.

Director Gyan Mukherjee's 'Kismet' in 1943 ran successfully for 187 weeks. It was a runaway success and one of the biggest box-office hits in the history of Indian cinema. He played the role of a chain-smoker and it was a negative character. No hero would have agreed to play such a negative role in the beginning of his film career. 'Kangan', 'Bandhan', 'Jhoola' and 'Naya Sansar' were his very successful films. Bombay Talkies' 'Majboor' ran to packed houses to become a jubilee hit.

Ashok Kumar with others founded Filmistan in 1943 and produced successful films under this banner. He did 'Najma', 'Chal Chal re Naujawan' in 1944, 'Begum' in 1945, 'Shikari', 'Humayun', 'Howrah Bridge' and 'Ziddi' in 1948. In the last film he introduced his brother as a musician. Director Kamaal Amrohi's 'Mahal' Ashok Kumar with the ethereal beauty Madhubala in 1949 became a super hit. 'Mashal' in 1950 was based on the story of Bankim Chandra Chatterjee and proved a hit. After severing his relations with Bombay Talkies in 1954, he started his own Ashok Kumar Productions and produced 'Samaj' but it flopped. He made three more films but all of them failed miserably. He produced 'Parineeta' and acted opposite Meena Kumari. It was directed by Bimal Roy and proved very successful. Subsequently he had to close down his production company and take to full-time acting after a gap of three years.

He went to Calcutta and performed in some Bengali films. His Hindi films 'Samadhi', 'Deedar', 'Afsana' and 'Sangram' were hits at box-office and put him again on the track of a successful actor. On the insistence of Nutan, he did a role in 'Bandini' in 1963. It was an interesting film but an out and out Nutan film. 'Meri Surat Teri Ankhen' was a unique experience for him as he had to blacken his face and look ugly for the role. His other films — 'Oonche Log', 'Mamta', 'Ashirwaad', 'Satyakam', 'Adhikar' and 'Mere Mehboob' in 1963 were memorable films. Producer-director Kamaal Amrohi's film 'Pakeezah' was started in 1963 and was completed only in 1971. Ashok Kumar acted in this most successful film of its time and it became a landmark in the Indian film history. He did comic roles in 'Khatta-Meetha', 'Shaukeen', 'Victoria No. 203' and 'Chalti ka Naam Gaadi' — the last named with his two brothers, Anoop and Kishore. The film was considered one of the best comedy films. He did 'Bewafaa' with Raj Kapoor and Nargis. He acted in B.R. Chopra's film 'Kanoon' which was without any song and an experimental film.

He was conferred with the National Award for 'Gumrah' in 1963 and for 'Ashirwaad' in 1967. He was honoured with the Filmfare Lifetime Achievement Award in 1995. He presented episodes from TV serials 'Hum Log', 'Dada Dadi ki Kahani' and acted in B.R. Chopra's TV serial 'Bahadur Shah Zafar'. He had a good number of successful films to his credit.

Ashok Kumar was a painter, homoeopath, astrologer, boxer, chess-player, singer and above all, a good companion and a kind human being. He died at the age of ninety years after a prolonged illness on 10th December 2001 at Bombay. His career spanned nearly seven decades.

* * *

Amitabh Bachchan

Amitabh Bachchan, the legendary icon and the 'Shahenshah' of Bollywood today is an international celebrity. He rules the hearts of the people right from Kashmir to Kanyakumari. He is an actor, anchor, presenter, announcer, drama artiste, producer and above all, a social and family man. He was born on 11 October 1942 in Allahabad during the days of India's freedom struggle. He is the son of Teji Bachchan and father Harivash Rai Bachchan, a well-known poet. He did graduation from Kirorimal College of Delhi University after studying at Sherwood College in Nainital. His memories of the school still haunt him. He acted in plays at both school and college. Before joining the film world in 1968, he worked in Calcutta with Shaw Wallace as an executive.

His entry into Bollywood was not easy. He was spurned by filmmakers because he was lean, thin, with unconventional looks and unusually tall with a height of six feet and three inches. His voice was rough and tough. He also did not qualify the audition test of All India Radio then. Only through his father's connection to director K.A. Abbas that he got the first break in the film 'Saat Hindustani' in 1969. But this film was an utter failure.

Amitabh then acted in 'Parwana' in which he played the role of a villain, 'Bombay to Goa' and in two films with Jaya Bhaduri in 1972 --- 'Bansi Birju' and 'Ek Nazar'. 'Zanjeer' in 1973 in which he acted opposite Jaya Bhaduri was the thirteenth film and it became a turning point in his life and won him the title of 'the angry young man'. The role played by him was of a hard and harsh police officer. It was during this period that Amitabh and Jaya Bhaduri got drawn to each other and they ultimately married soon afterwards on 3 June 1973. He was thirty-one years old and Jaya was twenty-five. It was however producer-director Sunil Dutt who gave him a chance in his film 'Reshma aur Shera' in 1971 in which he played a small but significant role of his life as a mute man. He then played the lead role for the first time in his career in 'Pyaar ki Kahani' in 1971 opposite Tanuja. His artistic calibre was noticed in Hrishikesh Mukherji's film 'Anand' in 1970. He was eclipsed by a stellar performance from Rajesh Khanna but won the award for Best Supporting Actor for the role of Babu Moshai. The film was a very successful hit and they worked together in 'Abhimaan', 'Chupke Chupke', 'Mili', 'Sholay' and 'Silsila' in 1981.

His career further took off when he first started working with the dusky beauty Rekha in 'Do Anjaane' in 1976, but his film 'Namak Haram' in 1973 was released first. He won the award for Best Supporting Actor. They became known as the most successful romantic pair in Bollywood. Their memorable films were 'Do Ajnabi' in 1976, 'Alaap' in 1977, 'Imaan Dharam' in 1977, 'Khoon Pasina', 'Muqaddar ka Sikander' in 1978, 'Mr Natwar Lal' and 'Suhaag' in 1979.

Producer G.P. Sippy's multi-starrer film 'Sholay' and director Yash Chopra's 'Deewar' proved super hits, mainly because of Amitabh Bachchan. Both the films were full of violence and action drama. He further proved his acting calibre in Manmohan Desai's film 'Amar Akbar Anthony' in 1977, 'Don' in 1978, 'Agneepath' in 1990 and 'Hum' in 1991. He won awards for these films. He was conferred the National Film Award for Best actor for 'Agneepath' in 1990.

Once again he worked with Prakash Mehra in his box-office hit film 'Hera Pheri' in 1975,

'Muqaddar ka Sikander' in 1979, 'Lawaaris' in 1981, 'Namak Halal' in 1982 and 'Sharaabi' in 1984. Films like 'Trishul' in 1978 and 'Kala Patthar' in 1979 further cemented his image as an angry man. His romantic image was presented in Yash Chopra's hit films — 'Kabhi Kabhi' in 1976 and 'Silsila' in 1981 — the latter being a kind of biographical love story. In Ramesh Sippy's 'Shakti' in 1982 his acting prowess was placed against that of veteran Dilip Kumar. Director Manmohan Desai's blockbuster 'Coolie' in 1983 proved unlucky for him as he met with a serious accident and had to be hospitalised. He acted in other hits like 'Parvarish', 'Naseeb' in 1981, 'Desh Premee' and 'Mard' in 1985.

After Indira Gandhi's assassination in 1984, he contested the General Election for the first time from Allahabad, his hometown, and he won. But politics got him trapped in scandals and so he resigned from the membership of Parliament. Politics was not his cup of tea.

He acted in 'Khuda Gawah' in 1992 with Sridevi and in 'Insaniyat' in 1993 with Jayaprada. This was his eighty-sixth film and he became a legend in Indian cinema. Amitabh remained away from films for about five years to nurse his production house called Amitabh Bachchan Corporation Limited (ABCL) as it had run neck deep into debt. So he had to revert back to the silver screen once again. He came back to films in 1997 with 'Mrityudata' followed by 'Mohabbaatein', 'Ek Rishta', 'Aks', 'Kabhi Khushi Kabhi Gham', 'Hum Kissise Kam Nahin', 'Aankhen' and 'Kaante'. He tried his luck on the small screen and anchored the programme entitled 'Kaun Banega Crorepati' and the show created history on the Indian television. With earnings from the television programmes and modelling assignments, he paid off the debt and the heavy amount of income-tax imposed on him.

He played in 'Kyon Ho Gaya Na', 'Hum Kaun Hain', 'Veer Zara' and 'Ab Tumhare Hawale Watan Sathiyon' released in 2004. He put in a brilliant performance with Rani Mukherjee in award-winning film 'Black' in 2005. He acted in 'Veer Zara' — a super hit film.

Besides acting in ad campaigns and films, he was appointed UNICEF's goodwill ambassador because of his enormous popularity.

Recently he fell ill and had to be hospitalised for abdomen surgery. He has become an icon in the film world and is one of the busiest stars of Bollywood. He was conferred the Padma Bhushan on 26 January 2001 for his outstanding contributions to Indian cinema. He has won several Filmfare awards as also Lifetime Achievement Awards. Internationally he was termed the Superstar of the Millennium in an online poll on BBC. His wax statue is installed in Madame Tussaud's Wax Museum in London.

* * *

Aamir Khan

The actor Aamir Khan, the second child of producer-father Tahir Husain and mother Zeenat Husain was born on 14 March 1965 in Holy Family Hospital, Bandra in Bombay. In his young age he was interested in tennis and used to play with the kids of the building. He became the state tennis champion for Maharashtra. His brother Faisal and sisters Nikhat and Farhat used to play in his team. He hated studies but loved to go to school. Who could have known at that time that this little, charming and chocolate-faced boy would become a leading star of Indian cinema. Since childhood he was a team man, supportive and patient. Since he hailed from a filmmaker's family and his uncle Nasir Husain was a leading film producer-director, he was introduced as a child artiste in Nasir Husain's film 'Yaadon ki Baraat' in 1973. When he was young he wanted to join the Pune Film Institute but his father advised him to join his uncle Nasir Husain to learn all about the film business. He assisted him as assistant director on the sets of 'Manzil Manzil' and 'Zabardast'. After a gap of ten years, he also assisted director Ketan Mehta in the making of the film 'Holi' in 1983 and performed a short role in it. Meanwhile he fell in love with the girl next door and proposed to her the day he turned twenty-one. But there was opposition to the marriage since he was a Muslim and the girl Reena Datta hailed from a Hindu family and was the daughter of the regional manage of Air India. So they eloped and got married secretly in a registered marriage. He has a son Junaid and daugher Aira. He is an emotional and passionate person.

When producer Nasir Husain found that his films were not running well, he decided to launch Aamir in his next project 'Qayamat se Qayamat Tak' in 1988 with Juhi Chawla in the lead. The film based on a tragic love story and provided with catchy music turned out to be a blockbuster and at the age of twenty-three, Aamir became a new star. Subsequently he worked in films like 'Raakh', 'Love Love Love', 'Awwal Number', 'Diwana Mujhsa Nahin', 'Dil Hai ke Manta Nahin' in 1991 and 'Jo Jeeta Wohi Sikander' in 1992 further cementing his hero's image in Bollywood. He displayed a natural flair for comedy in 1993 with his film 'Hum Hain Rahi Pyaar ke' and in Rajkumar Santoshi's film 'Andaaz Apana Apana' in 1994. By then he had reduced his workload in acting in not more than three films a year. His transition from a teen idol to a mature adult came with the Hindi adaptation of 'Kramer vs Kramer' and called 'Hum Akele Tum Akele' in 1995. Aamir, who had become a father in real life, said that his experience with son Junaid helped him in assaying the role of a 'single' father with reality.

In the film 'Baazi' in 1995, Aamir performed the role of a woman and while taking off his costume, his skin came off but he continued with the shooting. In Ram Gopal Verma's film 'Rangeela' in the same year, he acted with Urmila Matondkar as a tapori and it became a super hit film. The film 'Ishq' in 1997 with Ajay Devgan and 'Raja Hindustani' in 1996 had an intimate kiss scene with Karishma Kapoor. In 1998 the film 'Ghulam' with Rani Mukherjee as the leading lady proved a box-office super hit film and so did its song 'Aati kya Khandala…'

Today he is one of the topmost stars of Bollywood. He feels that working continuously in a number of films at one time is not an ideal way of working. He has decided to work in one film at a time so that he can concentrate with single-minded devotion on each film. He worked as a police officer in

'Sarfarosh', as a taxi-driver in 'Raja Hindustani', as Romeo in 'Dil Chahta Hai' and as Bhuvan in 'Lagaan' in 2001. A seasoned artiste, he slowly turned to production with the film 'Lagaan' which became India's official entry to the Oscar. It also got nominated among the first five films for the Filmfare Best Film Award and he won the Filmfare Best Actor Award for his performance in 'Raja Hindustani'.

Aamir abides by what he says. According to him, hard work, commitment and team work always help him in filmmaking. He performed brilliantly in the period film 'Mangal Pandey' in 2005 with Rani Mukherjee and then in 'Rang de Basanti' in 2006. Both the films were hits and further established his image as one of the greatest and dedicated, disciplined and top stars of the Indian cinema. At a recent press conference he made two very pertinent observations: the Indian youth of today should appreciate the importance of India's development and hopes that the Hindi film industry would become the best in the world.

Agreed he is from a family background related to Hindi cinema, it is his talent and hard work that have earned him the slot where he is today. Using the classic 'method acting' style, Aamir has acted in all genres of films— comedy, action, drama and romance. He is intense, invigorating and inspirational in his acting. Of late, he has shifted his attention from reel life to real life and he joined the Narmada Bachao Andolan *dharna* led by Medha Patkar on 14 April 2006 at Jantar Mantar, New Delhi to support the affected people.

In 2002, he divorced his first wife Reena from whom he has had two children and got married to Kiran Rao in January 2006. He is planning to produce his next untitled film.

* * *

Abhishek Bachchan

Abhishek Bachchan was completely raw when he started his film career. Though his father Amitabh Bachchan and mother Jaya Bachchan are veteran celebrities of the silver screen, and he had ample opportunity to watch them work and act in films, he did not become a successful star overnight. He was born in 1976. He has a sister Sweta Nanda who is married and has two children.

On reaching adulthood, he wanted to act in films. His debut film was director J.P. Dutta's '*Refugee*' in 2001 with debutant actress Kareena Kapoor, the grand daughter of the late Raj Kapoor. It was a love story set against the backdrop of partition. He started his career under the guidance of his father Amitabh and director J.P. Dutta polished his acting qualities. The film '*Refugee*' registered his presence in Bollywood and caught the attention of filmmakers. The first film in which he helped as a production boy was '*Major Saab*'.

He entered the industry because he wanted to do so. He had to go through some rough time and worked hard to succeed. He is sincere, devoted and earnest with no image to live up to. He has to create his own image and place. His earlier films were far from successful. He did those films mainly because he liked the scripts. He acted with Aishwarya Rai in '*Dhai Akshar Prem Ke*' in 2000, '*Bas Itna sa Khwab Hai*' in 2001 with Rani Mukherjee, '*Haan Maine Bhi Pyaar Kiya*' in 2002 with Karishma Kapoor and '*Main Prem ki Deewani Hoon*' in 2003 with Kareena Kapoor. On acting with successful actresses, his career took off. His film '*Zameen*' in 2003 was an out and out action film. His '*Run*' in 2004 was a remake of the Tamil film. In J.P. Dutta's film '*LoC–Kargil*' in 2003, he played the role of an army officer and the film was based on the Kargil war.

Abhishek keeps watching his own movies to find out in which department he is weak so that he can further improve. His films '*Run*', '*Yuva*', '*Rakh*' and '*Naach*' flopped at the box-office in 2004. '*Dhoom*' with Esha Deol proved to be a successful film. He won the Filmfare Award for Best Supporting Actor in the film '*Yuva*'. Both he and his father featured together in '*Bunty aur Babli*' and in '*Sarkar*' in 2005. It was exciting for him to co-star with his father. The film '*Sarkar*' was a serious film and became his first hit film. '*Bunty aur Babli*' was an out and out fun film and the ramp song of the film in which he acted with his father became most popular; Aishwarya Rai gave a dance performance in a special appearance. The song '*Kajrare kajrare…*' became a hit song. His film '*Dus*' with Sanjay Dutt and Esha Deol did average business and '*Naach*' in 2004 was an artistically made film. He made small but commendable appearances in '*Hum Tum*' in 2004 and in '*Salaam Namaste*' in 2005. In the film '*Neal n Nikki*' in 2005 he made a special appearance and in '*Bluff Master*' in 2005, with Priyanka Chopra, he did a successful role. He sang a beautiful ramp song in it that became a popular number.

Abhishek has acted successfully in a Bengali film '*Desh*' in 2002 in which he played as Jaya Bachchan's son but spoke not a single sentence in Bengali. His second Bengali film was '*Antarmahal: Views of the Inner Chamber*' in 2005 in which he played the role of a Bihari sculptor. He has some more films and important projects on hand. According to him, he has never wanted to do anything else but be an actor. So the show goes on…

* * *

Aishwarya Rai

Born on 1 November 1973 in a traditional family at Mangalore in Karnataka, Aishwarya was nicknamed Ash, Aishu, Gullu and today she is called the 'queen of Bollywood'. Her father is Krishnaraj, a merchant navy officer and her mother Vrinda Rai is a housewife. She has a brother Aditya who is three years older than her. She moved to Mumbai at the age of four with her father. She appeared in the ICSE examination but did not fare well. She passed Standard XI from Jai Hind College and Standard XII from D.V.G. Ruparel College. In her school days, she participated in games, yoga and dance. She received training in Bharatanatyam and also learnt Hindustani and Carnatac music. She started modelling at a young age when she was in Standard IX in school at Arya Vidhya Mandir, Santa Cruz, Mumbai for Camlin Industries.

She won the Ford Supermodel Contest in 1991 and appeared in the same year on the cover of *Vogue* magazine. She modelled for Palmolive and became known as the Palmolive girl. She is a brand star for Nakshatra diamonds, De Beers diamonds, Garden sarees besides appearing in ad campaigns for Pepsi and Coke. She is currently ambassador for Longines watches since 1999 and loves collecting different types of watches. This gorgeous greenish-blue-eyed beauty can be seen popping out of her photographs in every market. During this period she was offered roles by leading filmmakers but she turned them down as she wanted to become an architect.

In 1994, she participated in the Femina Beauty Contest and was crowned Miss India runner-up and subsequently won the coveted Miss World title. The revered title brought in its wake a stream of offers from directors like Yash Chopra and Rajiv Rai, who had been wooing her even before she became a world beauty. She acted for the first time in Mani Ratnam's Tamil film '*Iruvar*' in 1996. Perhaps it was the attraction of working with Mani Ratnam or the challenge of a double role that she acquiesced and agreed to grace the silver screen with her presence. Director Rahul Rawail presented her in 1997 in his film '*Aur Pyaar Ho Gaya*' opposite Bobby Deol and for that she was conferred the Screen Best Female Debutant Award. The film however was written off by critics and admirers alike.

Aishwarya began to be called the 'Jeans girl' after working in the Tamil film '*Jeans*' in 1998. The film did well in south India, but was a complete washout in its Hindi version. Such failures coupled with her drastic mistakes in judgement of films chosen did nothing for her. She found moderate applause for acting in movies like '*Aa ab Laut Chalein*'. Then came Subhash Ghai, a 'star maker' on the screen and he offered her the lead role in '*Taal*', which she grabbed with both hands. This time no one complained about her inclusion, as in a show of determination, she shut up her worst critics with an inspired performance. She even proved herself as a dancer of utmost grace and poise.

Her other film '*Devdas*' became the first Indian film to get a special screening at the Cannes Film Festival and she appeared at the premiere of this film in a coach draped in a scintillating mustard coloured saree. She even became the first Indian actor to be a member of the jury at the Cannes Film Festival. The year 2004 issue of *India Today* carried her photograph on its cover and the Time magazine listed her in the hundred Most Influential People in the World. She featured in the 2004

edition of the *Guinness Book of World Records*. She acted for the first time in the English film by Gurinder Chadha entitled '*Bride & Prejudice*' which was shot in London. She also became the first Indian female film star to be immortalised in wax at the world-famous Madame Tussaud's Wax Museum in London.

Sanjay Leela Bhansali's most ambitious remake '*Devdas*' in 2002 starring Aishwarya with Shah Rukh Khan and Madhuri Dixit broke all box-office records in India as well as in the USA. It created history in Bollywood. It was during the shooting of this film, that her ears began to bleed on wearing heavy earrings but that did not stop her from acting. She continued acting out her role as Paro, which she performed beautifully. In 2003, she acted in Rituparno Ghosh's Bengali film '*Chokher Bali*' and his Hindi film '*Raincoat*'. In 2003 she joined the elite L'Oreal dream team as its new international brand ambassador.

She ran in the Olympic torch relay in June 2004. Mattel released in 2005 a small number of Barbie dolls duly inspired by her and the entire lot was sold out in no time. A particular variety of the tulip flower has been named after her by the Dutch government.

Currently she is working in J.P. Dutta's film '*Umrao Jan*' with Abhishek Bachchan and in Ashutosh Gowariker's '*Jodha-Akbar*' opposite Hrithik Roshan. She even performed in the closing ceremony of the 2006 Commonwealth Games in Melbourne, Australia with 800 backup dancers accompanying her. She is today the beauty icon in many countries and not only in India.

* * *

Ajay Devgan

The versatile action hero-turned-romantic in one film and vice versa in another is none other than the sombre-faced Ajay Devgan, son of the renowned fight composer and director Veeru Devgan. He was born on 2 April 1967 and is married to the versatile and spontaneous heroine Kajol and has a daughter named Nysa.

The younger Devgan is competent enough to perform his own risky and dangerous action shots in films. In his childhood days he used to accompany his father to film shootings. He was not keen to become an actor then. But he would help in editing and also worked as assistant director at the age of nineteen with many filmmakers. All of a sudden, one day, director Kuku Kohli approached him to work in his film but Ajay refused. Ultimately he was persuaded to work in *'Phool aur Kaante'* and thereafter Ajay's life changed. This debut film of his in 1991 with actress Madhoo proved a smashing hit. He emerged with his first film as an action hero. His daring stunts and hair-raising fight scenes by riding two motorcycles at the same time left an everlasting image on the moviegoer's mind who felt that here was a man willing to fight his way through the wave of mushy romances that ruled the day. It overnight established him as a new star.

He is one of the topmost super stars of Bollywood. Filmmakers are keen to cast him in his films, because it ensures the box-office success of their films. He is the most dependable star-actor. He works hard in his films. He is always careful about the roles he chooses.

After *'Phool aur Kaante'*, Ajay performed in action films like *'Jigar'* in 1992, in *'Divyashakti'* in 1993 and in *'Vijaypath'* in 1994. These films cemented his stay in the film industry as a strong action hero. He worked in *'Bedardi'*, *'Dil hai Betaab'*, *'Ek hi Rasta'*, *'Sangram'*, *'Gundaraj'* and *'Hulchul'* in 1995. Somewhere in the middle of all the on-screen violence and breathtaking stunts, a less action role like that in *'Naajayaz'* in 1995 that of an illegitimate son of a gangster who becomes an upright police officer came his way.

The trend in his career took another turn when he worked in the film *'Ishq'* in 1997, a romantic love-comedy with Kajol. He switched from action hero to romantic hero with *'Pyar to Hona hi Tha'* in 1998 which was a big hit. He played a sentimental lover boy in *'Dilwale'* in 1994 and the film was very successful. Perhaps it was the success of these films or the desire to move away from the beaten track that prompted him to reduce his workload and concentrate on quality films. The film that allowed Ajay to come into his own as an actor was director Mahesh Bhatt's film *'Zakhm'* in 1998 and this earned him the first national Film Award for Best Actor. And then came the crowning glory of his successful foray into the commercial cinema it was Sanjay Bhansali's *'Dil de Chuke Sanam'* where he played a convincing role of a man who desperately tries to reunite his wife (Aishwarya Rai) with her former lover Salman Khan. The second National Film Award he got for the film *'The Legend of Bhagat Singh'* in 2003 and it is the highest form of recognition an actor can get. He has also earned two Filmfare awards.

In Raj Kumar Santoshi's film *'Khakee'* in 2004, he played the role of a cop with a dark shade, and this he had not done ever before. He has shown many faces in films --- the romantic hero in *'Chori*

Chori', a menacing underworld don in '*Company*', a killer in '*Deewangi*', a troubled husband in '*Bhoot*' while in '*Insaan*', in 2005, he played the role of one fighting against terrorism. He acted as a dacoit in the woman-oriented film '*Lajja*' and his film '*Qayamat*' was a hardcore action film. Director Prakash Jha's '*Gangajal*' based on corruption between bureaucracy and politics had him acting as an idealistic cop who weeds out corruption. He acted as a police official in '*Blackmail*' in 2004 with Priyanka Chopra. It proved an average film. His film, '*Company*' pushed up his rank in the film world. Though '*Bhoot*' was not successful in cities, but at small centres, the film proved a hit. His performance in '*Hum Kisise Kam Nahin*' in 2002 was a balanced role and was appreciated by one and all. Director Rituparno Ghosh's first Hindi film '*Raincoat*' in 2004 with Aishwarya Rai was a mediocre film but Ajay's superb performance was well acclaimed. His film '*Kaal*' in 2005 and produced by Shah Rukh Khan was also an average film. But a very challenging role was performed by him in Harry Baweja's film '*Main Aisa hi Hoon*' in 2005 with Sushmita Sen and Esha Deol. He also worked in '*Insaan*', '*Tarzan the Wonder Car*', '*Zameer*', '*Masti*', '*Shikhar*' and '*Apharan*' in 2005 with Bipasha Basu. He has many films on hand.

He even produced two films: '*Hindustan ki Kasam*' in 1999 and '*Raju Chacha*' in 2000 but both these films were loosing propositions. Today his company, The Devgan Entertainment & Software Limited produces films and programmes for television, etc.

* * *

Anil Kapoor

Anil Kapoor was born on 24 December 1959 in Bombay. He studied at St. Xavier's College and is married to Sunita Bhambani. He has a son and two daughters. He has one sister Reena and two brothers — producer Boney Kapoor and actor Sanjay Kapoor.

It was but natural for him to be attracted to the film world because his father Surinder Kapoor was a renowned filmmaker. Thus acting has been sort of in his blood. He played an important but a very small role in director Umesh Mehra's multi-starrer film 'Hamare Tumhare' in 1979 with Sanjeev Kumar and Rakhee. He again acted a small role in Tarachand Barjatya's film 'Ek Baar Kaho' in 1980 when he was noticed by filmmakers. Producer Surinder Kapoor, his father, introduced him in the lead role in his debut film in 'Woh Saat Din' in 1983 opposite Padmini Kolhapure. He performed the role of an innocent and simple rustic called Pem Pratap Patialewala who visits the city for the first time. His acting was influenced by that of Raj Kapoor. Producer-director Yash Chopra was impressed by his performance and made him act in 'Mashaal' in 1984 opposite Dilip Kumar. It was a hit film. He became a multi-faceted star. He won the Filmfare Award for the Best Supporting Actor for 'Mashaal'. Then he acted in Sawan Kumar Tak's film 'Laila' but it flopped. He played a variety of roles in different films within a span of four years and these films were 'Saheb', 'Itihaas', 'Love Marriage', 'Yudh' and 'Pyaar Kiya Hai Pyaar Karenge'. He played a romantic hero in 'Mohabbatein' and an angry young man in 'Insaaf ki Aawaz'.

He became a super star with the success of Subhash Ghai's film 'Karma' in 1986 and producer-brother Boney Kapoor's 'Mr India' in 1987 opposite heroine Sridevi. Simultaneously his films 'Tejaab' in 1988 opposite Madhuri Dixit, 'Eashwar' in 1988, 'Rakhwala' in 1989, 'Ram Lakhan' in 1989 and 'Lamhe' in 1991 became super hit films. His one song 'My name is Lakhan…' became very popular. In 'Eashwar' he brilliantly portrayed the role of a mentally challenged youth and it was a rather negative role. He became a sought after star of Bollywood when he played the role of a freedom fighter in '1942 A Love Story' in 1998.

Anil won the Filmfare Award for Best Actor for 'Tejaab' in 1988 and 'Beta' in 1992 as well as the Critics Award for 'Virasat'. His other successful films are 'Mann', 'Biwi No.1', 'Gharwali Baharwali', 'Judaai', 'Heer Ranjha', 'Taal' and the most memorable film of his is 'Roop ki Rani Choron ka Raja' of 1993. He acted a difficult role in 'Lajja' too in 2001. He won the National Film Award for the film 'Pukar' in 2000. His recent successful films are 'Musafir' in 2004, 'Bewafaa', 'My Wife's Murder', 'Chocolate' in 2005, 'Hum ko Deewana Kar Gaya' in 2006. His film 'No Entry', a powerful, glamorous and entertaining film, proved one of the most successful films for the year 2005. He has cut down on his acting assignments but is known as a dependable star among the filmmakers.

* * *

Dev Anand

The legendary film icon was conferred with Dada Saheb Phalke Award for the year 2002 for his outstanding contribution to the Indian film industry. He found the award stimulating and energising. He could not help feeling excited like a child. Probably that has helped him to stay young for so long. Called a romantic hero, he is an evergreen thespian. He has developed his own style and dress code and maintains an individualistic style that has endeared him to three generations of the masses. He is around eighty-three-years old and has never thought about leaving either filmmaking or the industry. He intends to make films called '*Beauty Queen*' and '*Song of Life*'. He has always made films on contemporary issues.

Devdutt Pishorimal Anand was born on 26 September 1923 in a well-to-do advocate family at Gurdaspur, a small town in Punjab. His father Kishori Lal Anand was an eminent lawyer. He is the sixth sibling among nine brothers and sisters. His other well-known brothers were Chetan Anand and Vijay Anand, both of whom are no longer alive. He did graduation in English literature from Government College, Lahore and reached Bombay on 19 July 1944 in search of employment with a mere thirty rupees in his pocket.

In his early days, he worked for some time with the Military Censor Office on a salary of one hundred sixty-five rupees per month. His job was to read letters written by soldiers to their families. When jobless, he acted in some plays produced by the IPTA. His debut film, Prabhat's '*Hum Ek Hain*' in 1946 was an average film. His next film by Famous Pictures '*Mohan*' did not do anything for him. He came into limelight with the success of Bombay Talkies '*Ziddi*' in 1948 by acting opposite Kamini Kaushal. It was a hit film. During his stay at Prabhat Studios, Poona he became friendly with Guru Dutt and promised to take him as director if he ever produced a film in future. He joined hands with his brother Chetan Anand and floated his own production company by the name of Navketan Studios in 1949. He honoured his commitment and made Guru Dutt to direct Navketan's '*Baazi*' in 1951 starring Geeta Bali and Kalpana Kartik. The film was a big hit and he attained stardom. Prior to the film '*Baazi*' he had already worked as a hero in films '*Vidya*' in 1948, '*Jeet*' in 1949, '*Shair*' and '*Afsar*' in 1949, '*Neeli*' in 1950 with Suraiya. During this period he got attracted to Suraiya but could not marry her due to objections raised by Suraiya's maternal grandmother. Later he got married during the lunch break while shooting for '*Taxi-driver*' with the heroine of six of his films, Kalpana Kartik alias Mona, in 1954. She is a Christian by birth. The film was directed by his brother Chetan Anand. He has two children daughter named Devina and son Suneil.

Some of his most memorable films are '*Munimji*' made in 1955, '*Taxi-driver*' in 1954, '*CID*' in 1956, '*Paying Guest*', '*Nau Do Gyaraah*' in 1957, '*Love Marriage*', '*Kala Paani*', '*Hum Dono*', '*Tere Ghar ke Saamne*', '*Guide*', '*Jewel Thief*', '*Johnny Mera Naam*' in 1970, '*Des Pardes*' in 1978, '*Prem Pujari*' in 1970, '*Sau Crore*' in 1993, '*Main Solah Baras Ki*' in 1998, '*Censor*' in 2001 and '*Love at Times Square*' in 2003. With the continued success of his films, he became the most sought after star and filmmaker. His film '*Hare Rama Hare Krishna*' in 1971 dealt with the theme

of hippies and drug addicts and was beautifully shot for the first time in Nepal. It proved a hit film. He played the role of a smuggler in 'Jaal', as member of a gang in 'Dushman', an urban orphan in 'Funtoosh', a pickpocket in 'Pocketmaar', an inspector in 'CID', a black-marketer in 'Kaala Bazaar', a killer in 'Bombay ka Babu' and in a double role in 'Hum Dono' in 1961. 'Guide' in 1965 was one of the most successful films due to its songs, music, story and picturisation and became a milestone in Indian cinema. He became director, producer and actor with the film 'Prem Pujari' in 1970 and produced a good number of films. His last film was 'Mr Prime Minister' in 2005.

Dev Anand was conferred the Filmfare Award as Best Actor for 'Kala Paani' and 'Guide'. He was awarded the Padma Bhushan in 2001 by the government. His films have won five national and various state-level awards. He has won recognition and honour not only in India but abroad too for his contributions to Indian cinema. In 1993 he was presented the Raj Kapoor Trophy at the thirty-eighth Filmfare Award function as well as being honoured with the Thirteenth Express Cinema Award in Madras and Canada for his lifetime contributions to cinema. In 1996, during the shooting in Scotland of his film 'Main Solah Baras Ki', he was honoured by the Scotland Council there. He is known for introducing new faces in his films like Zeenat Aman, Tina Munim, Natasha and Sophia Chikra. He has not given up yet and hopes to produce more films. Unconcerned if his films succeed or fail, he starts planning for the other even before he has completed the shooting for one. According to him the process of filmmaking is more exciting than the fate of the film. He has proved the most enduring horse of the race with most of his contemporaries no longer alive, except for Dilip Kumar.

* * *

Dharmendra

Macho-man Dharam Singh Deol alias 'Garam Dharam' or Dharmendra was born on 8 December 1935 at Phagwara in Punjab. He was married to Prakash Kaur at the age of nineteen. Initially he worked with a tubewell-boring firm, American Drilling Company, for some time. He hails from a north Indian Punjabi family. He has the looks of a gentleman, the body of a he-man and when it comes to acting in films, he has been great.

He was fascinated with the bioscope since his childhood. During those days touring bioscopes moved from town to town. Once he went to see director A.R. Kardar's film *'Dillagi'* starring Suraiya and Shyam. He was so impressed with this film that he saw it a number of times. One day, he spotted an advertisement of Filmfare Spot the Talent Contest and went to Bombay to attend it. Fortunately he was selected and given the chance to act in a film. His debut film was *'Railway Platform'* in 1955 and was directed by Ramesh Saigal. For a further period of five years he struggled in Bolywood till he got a chance in Arjun Hingorani's film *'Dil Bhi Tera Hum Bhi Tere'* in 1960. His film *'Shola aur Shabnam'* in 1961 was a romantic love story but he got appreciation and recognition in the following women-oriented films: *'Anpadh'* in 1962 wherein he acted opposite Mala Sinha and in *'Bandini'* in 1963 where in he acted in a supporting role with Nutan and Ashok Kumar. He worked in a multi-starrer film based on war and directed by Chetan Anand the film *'Haqeeqat'* in 1964. But he got recognition as a he-man after working in O.P. Ralhan's *'Phool aur Patthar'* in 1966 with Meena Kumari in the lead and he was by now a star. The film was successful at the box-office. He worked with her in a number of films and reached great heights in Bollywood. His masculine image lured the producers and got him signed to work in their films. By now he was a busy star.

He displayed a great penchant for acting serious roles. He performed in director Hrishikesh Mukherjee's films *'Manjhli Didi'* in 1967 and *'Satyakam'* in 1969. His action-hero image was established with the films *'Aankhein'* in 1968, *'Mera Gaon Mera Desh'* in 1971, *'Jugnu'* in 1973, *'Kahani Kismet Ki'* in 1973, *'Yaadon ki Baraat'* in 1978, and subsequently *'Charas'*, *'Azad'* and *'Sholay'* in 1975.

The film *'Sholay'* proved a super-duper film and became a milestone in the history of Bollywood. His role and performance as Veeru became unforgettable. His only drawback was he could not dance to save his soul and would emphatically say 'no' to a dance number despite being famous as a 'yes' man to anything that was suggested to him. *'Sholay'* was highly successful at the box-office with Hema Malini acting opposite him and she subsequently acted with him in films like *'Naya Zamana'* in 1971, *'Raja Jani'*, *'Seeta aur Geeta'* in 1972, *'Jugnu'* and *'Dost'* in 1974, *'Razia Sultan'* in 1983. They had worked in about 28 films together. Hema Malini fell in love with him and got married to him despite the fact that he was already married. Later she gave birth to two daughters, Esha and Ahana and presently Esha too is working in films and has established herself very well.

Dharmendra also tried his hand at producing films and produced two films: *'Betaab'* in 1983 with Amrita Singh and *'Barsaat'* in 1995 with Twinkle Khanna to launch his sons; Sunny and Bobby.

He remained on top in the film world of Bollywood for about three decades. During his heydays, he worked in some memorable films like 'Chupke Chupke', 'Dharamveer', 'Shalimar', 'The Burning Train', 'Professor', 'Hakumat', 'Hatyara', 'Ghulami', 'Kshatriya' and 'Sultan' in 2000. He also produced 'The Legend of Bhagat Singh' featuring both his sons.

In his entire film career he did not get any award either for his successful films or for his acting. But lately, in 1997, he was awarded the Filmfare Lifetime Achievement Award for his contribution to Hindi cinema. Presently he is a Member of Parliament from Bikaner (Rajasthan) and fought the election on behalf of the Bharatiya Janata Party. Hema Malini is also a Member of Parliament nominated to the Rajya Sabha. They are leading a happy married life.

* * *

Dilip Kumar

Dilip Kumar

Dilip Kumar or the 'tragedy king' of Hindi cinema was born on 11 December 1922 in a Pathan family at Peshawar (now in Pakistan). Dilip's father moved with his family to Deolali and then finally to Bombay. As a fruit-seller's son, who once successfully ran a British Army canteen in Pune, Dilip rose to become one of the greatest stars of the Indian cinema.

The golden era of Indian cinema had already begun when the legendary Dilip Kumar alias Yusuf Khan appeared on the silver screen through Bombay Talkies' film '*Jwar Bhata*' in 1944. He was given the name Dilip Kumar by noted Hindi author Bhagwati Charan Verma. He could not prove his mettle in '*Jwar Bhata*' or in '*Pratima*' in 1945 or in '*Milan*' in 1946 as his roles were insignificant.

Dilip was young, smart but shy and reserved in nature when he joined the industry. His style of dialogue delivery with frequent pauses was appreciated by most of the cine-goers. Melody queen, Noorjehan, teamed with him in Shaukat Hussein's '*Jugnu*' in 1947 and that gave him the courage to perform better. He got an opportunity to work with Nargis in Ambika Films' '*Anokha Pyaar*' and in Wadia Films' '*Mela*' in 1948. Music director Naushad composed the music of '*Mela*' and because of him its songs and melodious music became popular in those days. Songs like '*Yeh zindagi ke mele duniya mein kam na honge…*' and others were hummed by thousands of people. Simultaneously Filmistan Studio produced two films: '*Nadia ke Paar*' and '*Shaheed*' in 1948 with heroine Kamini Kaushal. Music director Gulam Haider composed such impressive and heart-rending music for '*Shaheed*' that cine-goers would weep in the cinema halls on hearing the song '*Watan ki raah mein watan ke naujawan shaheed ho…*' during the death procession of the hero in the film. Dilip Kumar brilliantly portrayed the role of Shaheed and became the loved star of the masses. Moreover during the same period, India had won Independence at the cost of the lives of many freedom fighters. The brutalities of the British were shown in this film and it drew surging crowds to see it. Dilip Kumar fell in love with Kamini Kaushal in this period but she left him heart-broken.

Dilip became known as the '*tragedy king*' after working in films like '*Mela*' in 1948 with Nargis, '*Andaaz*' in 1949 with Nargis and Raj Kapoor, with Kamini Kaushal in '*Babul*' in 1950, '*Deedar*' in 1951 with Nargis, '*Devdas*' in 1955 with Vyjayantimala and '*Udan Khatola*' in 1955 with Nimmi. These films were successful as well as hits due to their melodious music, story and superb lyrics. Naushad composed the music of '*Mela*', '*Andaaz*', '*Shabnam*', '*Babul*', '*Deeedar*', '*Aan*' and '*Udan Khatola*'.

On finding himself getting typecast due to acting in similar roles, he took to performing light-hearted roles. He showed his versatility of performance in the first colour film '*Aan*' in 1952 and then in '*Footpath*', '*Azad*', '*Insaniyat*', '*Naya Daur*', in 1957, '*Paigam*' and '*Kohinoor*' in 1960. His performances in '*Daag*', '*Amar*', '*Devdas*' and K.Asif's '*Mughal-e-Azam*' were landmark performances in the annals of Indian cinema. He not only played classic and serious roles successfully but also brilliantly performed comedy, action, romantic and melodramatic roles. Bimal Roy's popular musical '*Madhumati*' in 1958 proved most popular during those days. His song '*Suhana safar aur ye mausam hansi…*' and other songs from this film became hits.

Dilip produced a Bhojpuri film '*Ganga Jamuna*' in 1961 to play the role of an uneducated farmer, who becomes a dacoit in the latter part of the film. He won the Filmfare Award for this film. His films '*Dil Diya Dard Liya*', '*Aadmi*', '*Sanghursh*', '*Gopi*', '*Sagina*' and '*Bairaag*' did not do well at the box-office. In the film '*Musafir*', he not only acted but also sang a song '*Laagi nahin chhoote Rama&* ' which became very popular. For a short period he went into oblivion.

Dilip reappeared with powerful character roles such as in Manoj Kumar's '*Kranti*' in 1981, Ramesh Sippy's '*Shakti*' in 1982, '*Vidhata*', '*Karma*' and '*Saudagar*' in 1991, particularly with Rajkumar after a gap of about thirty-two years. He was well acclaimed for these roles. He was inspired to direct Sudhakar Bokade's film '*Kalinga*' for the first time but it did not mature and ultimately was shelved. Director Umesh Mehra's '*Qila*' in 1998 was an action film and he played the role of an elderly person in a befitting manner.

Dilip married on 11 October 1966, at the age of forty-four years, the then 'beauty queen' Saira Banu, daughter of actress Naseem Banu, star of yester years, who was aged twenty-two years. Her debut film was '*Junglee*' in 1961 and they have no children. Dilip married for the second time to Asma on 30 May 1980 but this marriage was short-lived and he divorced her on 22 June 1983.

During his career he won many prestigious awards including the Filmfare Award for '*Daag*', '*Azad*', '*Devdas*', '*Naya Daur*', '*Kohinoor*', '*Leader*', '*Ram aur Shyam*' and '*Shakti*' and this is a record. He is recipient of the Padma Bhushan, the Dada Saheb Phalke Award in 1995 and Nishan-e-Imtiaz by the Pakistan government in 1998. He was member of Rajya Sabha and was appointed Sheriff of Bombay in 1981. Presently he is leading a settled and satisfied life though he is not keeping good health.

* * *

Esha Deol

Esha Deol, an upcoming and budding actress, was born on 2 November 1982 to actor Dharmendra and actress Hema Malini. Her father, the macho-man Dharmendra, has been a versatile and successful actor besides being Member of Parliament from Bikaner. Her mother Hema Malini was known as the 'dream girl' and is a dance exponent besides being a Member of Parliament for the Rajya Sabha. Both her parents have touched the pinnacles of success in their careers during their time. Esha has yet to reach anywhere near them. She has a younger sister Ahana Deol. She is step-sister of successful stars, Sunny Deol and Bobby Deol. She has learnt Bharatanatyam and Odissi dances. She has performed with her mother and sister on various occasions in classical dance concerts.

Thus it was but natural for her to join the film industry because of her parents who have been involved with Bollywood since long. She has yet to reach the point where her parents had done during their time. Esha's debut film was *'Koi Mere Dil Se Pooche'* in 2002 and it was an average film. She has seen many ups and downs in her film career. Her early films like *'Na Tum Jaano Na Hum'*, *'Kyaa Dil ne Kahaa'* in 2002, *'Kuch to Hai'*, *'Chura Liya Hai Tumne'* in 2003 did not do well at the box-office. Initially she was not given much importance in the industry. She was termed a flop heroine. But during this period she learnt many things and became mature. She is grateful to her critics who have apprised her of her drawbacks and has become conscious about her looks. She has taken to wearing glamorous dresses and outfits. Her body language is attractive. She has worked in J.P. Dutta's film *'LoC-Kargil'*, a war film and in *'Yuva'* in 2004, registering her presence in Bollywood.

She became a successful star with the box-office hit *'Dhoom'* in 2004 with Abhishek Bachchan. Her glamorous looks, in particular her bewitching body postures, attracted the audience. Her role was beautifully picturised and the film became a hit. She has also worn bikinis and does not hesitate in doing such roles that expect her to reveal more than cover. She has worked according to the needs of the scripts of the films. She has been acclaimed for her roles in *'Kaal'* and *'Main Aisa Hi Hoon'* in 2005 with Ajay Devgan and Sushmita Sen. Her multi-starrer movies like *'No Entry'* and *'Shaadi No.1'* with Sanjay Dutt in 2005 or the comedy film like *'Pyaare Mohan'* in 2006 have proved successful and she has become a hot star in the film industry today. Her film *'Dus'* opposite Sanjay Dutt and Abhishek Bachchan were average films.

Producer Boney Kapoor's film *'No Entry'* in 2005 starring Anil Kapoor and Salman Khan was an entertainer and became the most successful film of the year. She is a very talented girl and has some good films in hand as these are under production awaiting release.

* * *

Guru Dutt

Intellectuals are born rarely. Guru Dutt Shiv Shanker Padukone was born on 9 July 1925 in Saraswat Brahamin family in Karnataka at Manglore. He was one of the most distinguished actor, director and producer of his time. He was an introvert. His impatient-ness was his creativity. He helped a lot in popularizing Indian cinema. His early education was held in Calcutta. During those days Calcutta and entire Bengal was facing the movements for social reconstruction and cultural proliferation. Guru Dutt was affected by these environments in his entire life. Sometimes he was termed as Bengali. He was not interested in routine education. After passing the class X in 1942 he left education. At the age of seventeen he left Calcutta and went to Almora to join Uday Shanker's Dance School. In this cultural centre Uday Shankar and his brother Ravi Shanker, the sitar maestro used to practice dance as well as impart coaching of music to students. He came to Poona in 1944 and joined Prabhat Studio to learn different aspects of filmmaking. He became assistant director in director Vishram Bedekar's film *Lakha Rani* in 1945, a year later and also acted in it as Lachman. At the age of twenty-one he was given the opportunity to display his calibre in P.L.Shantoshi's film *Hum Ek Hain* in 1946, as assistant and choreographer. He also appeared in it in a brief role. During his stay in Prabhat Studio he had an opportunity to work and learn different aspects of filmmaking from the best directors attached to the studio.

He reached Bombay in 1947 and worked as an assistant director to A.Banerjee of Famous Pictures. He worked as assistant director for film *Mohan* in 1947, as first assistant director to Amiya Chakravarty's film *Girls School* and subsequently in Gyan Mukherjee of Bombay Talkies film *Sangram* in 1950, as assistant director. During his stay at Prabhat he became very friendly with Devanand. Later on when Guru Dutt was twenty-six years old, he persuaded Devanand, who had already founded his own production concern in the name of Navketan, to produce a film *Baazi* in 1951, on the story duly written by him and Balraj Sahni. This film was directed by Guru Dutt independently. It was a successful film. He was also successful in breaking the popular image of a hero. Its songs, sung mainly by well-known playback singer, Geeta Roy, became a runaway hit like *Suno gahar kya gaaya& '*. The story and screenplay of film *Jaal* in 1952, for Filmarts was written by him. It was a story of a gold smuggler, duly directed by him but it was an average film. He did very small roles in these two films.

He married the renowned and popular singer Geeta Roy on 26 May 1953, who had sung many memorable, tuneful and popular songs for his films. She gave birth to two sons Tarun and Arun. Daughter Nina was born on 19 August, 1962 at Bombay.

He was of the opinion that presentation of ideas can be possible only when he could perform on the screen himself. Thus he became hero in *Baaz* in 1953, duly directed by him. He also wrote the story and screenplay of this film. It was a women-oriented film. He also floated his own production concern in the name of Guru Dutt Productions and directed its first film *Aar Paar* in 1954, with heroine Shyama. It was the story of a taxi-driver who loves the daughter of his taxi-owner. He established his image as a successful director with this hit film. He shot the songs in new style with

Westernised music in this film and instantly became popular. The next film he directed and produced 'Mr & Mrs 55' with Madhubala, who was known as the Venus of Hindi film world. It was a comedy film. Later on he produced a crime thriller 'C.I.D.' in 1956 with Dev Anand, Shakila and Johnny Walker and directed by Raj Khosla. He introduced south Indian beautiful dancer, Waheeda Rehman for the first time in this film. The film was successful at box-office all over India due to its music, songs and picturisation. His most memorable movie 'Pyaasa' in 1957, was the first directorial masterpiece by him. It was the story of a poet who was struggling to find recognition in the materialistic world. But a Call-girl got his poetry published and earned name and fame for him. The film reflected the relations between a writer and selfish publishers. It was a hit film because of its direction, tuneful music and popular songs. His performance was unique, memorable and powerful. The film became a classic milestone in the history of Indian cinema.

He produced, directed and performed in a biographical film 'Kaagaz ke Phool' in 1959 opposite Waheeda Rahman. It was the first cinemascope film in India. This unique and experimental film on serious issue was not liked by the masses. He was never discouraged from the failure of his films and continued to produce films. He produced a film with Muslim background 'Chaudhvin ka Chand' in 1960. The film was in black and white but two songs were shot in colour photography. It was an instant hit with its music and songs.

He performed in G.P. Sippy's film '12 O'clock' in 1958 with Waheeda Rehman was an average film. By this time Guru Dutt became more enthusiastic with the success of his films and decided to produce a multistarrer and mega budget film 'Sahib Bibi aur Ghulam' in 1962 on Bengali novel of Bimal Mitra on the feudal system. The performance of Meena Kumari as Chhoti Bahu was superb and memorable. He acted as the innocent Bhootnath. It was the story of a Bengali landlord family. It was a super hit at Box-Office. It's memorable, tuneful music and songs were popular and haunt today too. The film won the President's Silver Medal for its direction as well as the Film of the Year Award from BFJA. This was the last big film of his career. During the last three years of his career he worked in five films, directed and produced by others namely 'Sautela Bhai', 'Bahurani', 'Bharosa', 'Saanjh aur Savera', and 'Suhagan' in 1964. He also started some films but shelved them due to one reason or other. He also started producing 'Baharen Phir Bhi Aayengi' but could not complete it due to his untimely death. His brother Atmaram completed it by replacing Dharmendra in the lead role in 1966. Sanjeev Kumar replaced him in the role of Majnu in Producer-Director K. Asif's film 'Love & God' and the film was released in 1986.

His family life was not congenial but disturbed. On 10 October 1964 he was found dead in his apartment at the age of thirty-nine years. His estranged wife Geeta Dutt died on 20 July 1973. He will always be remembered as a classic and intelligent film director-producer.

* * *

country She even produced 'Swami' in 1977, 'Sharara' in 1984, 'Aawargi' in 1987 and 'Marg' in 1992, besides directing 'Dil Aashna Hai' in 1991 and 'Mohini' in 1994 for the TV. She also directed TV serials 'Noopur' in 1990 and 'Women of India' in 1996. She has played the role of Goddess Kali in Swami *Vivekananda* and *Jai Dakineshwari Kali*, films screened for the TV. She was awarded the Padma Shri in 2000. She has requested the government to construct a film museum in Mumbai.

After a gap of some years she again became active in acting. Her films 'Baghban' in 2003 and 'Veer Zara' in 2004 created records at the box-officer. Her performances in these two films are unforgettable. She has projected her lifetime's experience in these roles. She is still in great demand and some films are under way, though she is more keen to project her daughter Esha Deol on the screen. She is interested to work with Esha in a film though they have already danced together. Today she accepts films only when she is offered something worthwhile like 'Baghban'. She is of the view that it is not enough to be a beautiful celebrity; it is more important to use that power for furthering a social cause.

* * *

Hrithik Roshan

One fine day an idea cropped in the mind of father Rakesh Roshan who decided to produce an unusual film *Koi Mil Gaya* in 2003. He immediately rang up his son Hrithik, who was shooting for another film to find out his views about acting in his film. Hrithik willingly accepted to do the films. This offer came at a time when his career was under a cloud and as luck would have it, it proved to be a box-office hit. Hrithik's finely balanced performance of a mentally challenged boy with Preity Zinta was extraordinary particularly since this type of character had never been seen before in Hindi film. He was conferred the Filmfare Best Actor Award and Critic Award for the film. His debut film *Kaho Na Pyaar Hai* in 2000 with Amisha Patel was a super hit and this was highly commendable as it rarely happens that a debut film with a double role by the star becomes a box-office hit.

This film produced and directed by his father performed magic for the newcomer and was highly welcomed by the public, making the girls swoon on him. Overnight the boy who was an unknown entity to Bollywood had hit the headlines. Hrithik keeps a very low profile in real life and gives all praise to his father as the credit goes to Dad for presenting me so well. People say I have vindicated Dad by giving him the biggest hit of his career. I look at it a little differently. Dad has vindicated me by his hard work and his magic. The success has nothing to do with me. You'll have to see my other films to appreciate how hard Dad worked to bring the best out of me, said Hrithik in response to the praise showered on him. Soon after the release of this film, he became the superstar of Bollywood but this recognition came at a time when his father was shot at by a gang of gangsters. However, his father recovered soon and is hail and hearty now.

Hrithik Roshan with green eyes and nickname Duggu is the second child of father Rakesh Roshan and mother Pramila; he was born on 10 January 1974 at Mumbai. His grandfather Roshan was a renowned music composer and his uncle Rajesh Roshan is an established music director in his own right. His maternal grandfather J. Om Prakash was a successful film producer. His elder sister is named Sunaina. His wife is Suzanne, daughter of actor-producer Sanjay Khan and Zarine. He married her on 20 December 2000 after the successful release of his debut film, *Kaho Na Pyaar Hai*. They were in love with each other since Standard X in school. He studied at Bombay Scottish School and was a shy kid. He did his graduation in commerce from Sydenham College, Mumbai. During college, he actively participated in dance and music festivals. He is a good dancer and has leaned the techniques of filmmaking. He even worked as a child artiste in *Asha* in 1980 and danced with Jeetendra in a song *Jaane hum sadak ke logon se&* ' while acting in *Aap ke Deewane* in 1980 and in *Bhagwan Dada* in 1986 with Sridevi. For his first film *Aap ke Deewane* he was paid a mere Rs 300 for his role as a child.

During the making of the film *Khudgarz* in 1987, he worked for the first time as an assistant to his father Rakesh Roshan. He was assistant director for *King Uncle* in 1993 and associate director for *Karan Arjun* made in 1995, followed by *Koyla* in 1997. He also made the promos for the film *Koyla*.

After the box-office success of his debut film, none of his other films were successful till *Koi Mil Gaya* came his way. His films based on current burning issues like *Mission Kashmir* regarding the sensitive Kashmir problem and *Fiza* in 2000 with Karishma Kapoor on the Bombay riots and in which he

played the role of a fourteen-year old terrorist, emerged as routine commercial films. His film 'Yaadein' with Kareena Kapoor did not make much of a mark at the box-office. 'Kabhi Khushi Kabhi Gham' in 2001 was a blockbuster but helped him little. His films 'Aap Mujhe Achche Lagne Lage', 'Na Tum Jaano Na Hum' and 'Mujhse Dosti Karoge' in 2002 failed to click. Director Sooraj Barjatya's first flop film 'Main Prem ki Deewani Hoon' in 2003 based on the remake of his earlier film 'Chitchor' did not do much for his stature. Director Farhan Akhtar's film 'Lakshya' in 2004 with Preity Zinta and Amitabh Bachchan received a lukewarm response at the box-office from the public. It was the story of a confused young man, who joins the army to do some job and ends up becoming a war hero.

His biggest strength is his family. He is a much sought-after hero with filmmakers nowadays. He is of the view that he would like to do one film at a time. His home production 'Krrish' and 'Dhoom-2' have been released on the silver screen. His biggest quality is that he manages to remain unmoved by the media hype about him and has got his own speciality of differing from all other stars of Bollywood.

As far as his family life is concerned, he says he's very much looking forward to getting out of this phase and spend happy times with Mom, Dad, his wife Suzanne Khan and their newborn son.

* * *

Jaya Bachchan

Jaya Bachchan alias Jaya Bhaduri was born in 1948. She is the daughter of Tarun Bhaduri, a renowned journalist from Madhya Pradesh. While studying in a convent school in Bhopal, she received a telegram from Satyajit Ray asking her to act in his Bangla film 'Mahanagar' in 1962. Initially she was hesitant to work in a film. She had never thought of acting in films. Moreover she was not even allowed to go and see films and thus had no idea of this medium. Finally, she did come to act in this film at the age of thirteen years. She did two more Bangla films and in one entitled 'Dhannyi Meye', she acted as Uttam Kumar's sister. Only thereafter she was inclined towards this medium and joined the Pune Film Institute, though she had participated in plays and had some idea about how to act. She even learnt Bharatanatyam for five years. In 1966, she was conferred the Best NCC Cadet Award during the Republic Day parade. She was trained for two years at the Pune Film Institute and passed out with a gold medal.

Her debut film was director Hrishikesh Mukherjee's 'Guddi' in 1971 opposite Dharmendra and Sameet Bhanja. It was a successful film and she acted the role of a sober, simple, reserved and conservative girl, looking like a traditional Indian woman. She became a role model for new actresses during her time. While shooting for 'Guddi', she was signed for another film 'Uphaar' and by now she was a popular star.

Hrishikesh Mukherjee was responsible for making her team with Amitabh Bachchan whom she married when she was at the height of her career while he was a struggling newcomer. She worked jointly with Amitabh in 1972 in 'Bansi Birju' and in B.R. Ishara's 'Ek Nazar'. It was during this period that they began to court each other. They came close during the making of these films and ultimately married on 3 June 1973. He was thirty-one years old and she, twenty-five. In spite of being husband and wife, their pairing in films was very successful. They worked in 'Zanjeer', 'Abhimaan', 'Chupke Chupke', 'Mili', 'Sholay' and 'Silsila' in 1981. They paired once again in director Karan Johar's film 'Kabhi Khushi Kabhi Gham' in 2001.

Director-producer Prakash Mehra launched his production company with 'Zanjeer' in May 1973 and this became a super hit film. Their biggest hit till date has been producer G.P. Sippy's multi-starrer 'Sholay' in 1975 with Dharmendra, Sanjeev Kumar, Hema Malini and Amjad Khan. In this film she played the role of a widow displaying powerful emotions. Producer-director Yash Chopra's 'Silsila' was a kind of biographical love triangle and she received the Filmfare Award for 'Kora Kaagaz' and 'Naukar'.

Jaya was conferred her first Filmfare Award for Best Actress for her performance in 'Abhimaan' in 1973. The story of the film was inspired by the real life story of Geeta Dutt and Guru Dutt. She enjoyed working in 'Dil Deewana' and in 'Jawani Diwani' but the films did mediocre business. Her performances in 'Abhimaan', 'Kora Kaagaz', 'Mili', 'Koshish', 'Bawarchi', 'Naukar', 'Anamika', 'Shor' and 'Parichay' were widely acclaimed. When she was at the peak of her career, her son Abhishek and daughter Shweta were born, so she left working in films to look after them. Recently she even said that she cared more for her children than she did for her husband.

After about seventeen years of retired life, she made a comeback by playing a character role in Govind Nihalani's film *Hazaar Chaurasi ki Maa* in 1998. She later played an important role in *Fiza* in 2000 and it satisfied her. She once again brilliantly essayed the role of a mother in Karan Johar's melodrama *Kabhi Khushi Kabhi Gham* in 2001 opposite Amitabh Bachchan after a gap of about twenty years.

Her son Abhishek Bachchan has already joined films and is gaining popularity following his debut film *Refugee* with Kareena Kapoor. Her daughter Shweta Nanda is enjoying her married life and with her two children, a daughter Navya Naveli and son Agastya Nanda, she is living in New Delhi.

Jaya Bachchan had been a successful television producer and had served as chairperson of the National Centre of Films for Children and Young People. She was nominated to Rajya Sabha as Member of Parliament but on the Election Commission's recommendation, she was expelled on 17 March 2006 from Rajya Sbaha. She was disqualified on the ground that she held an office of profit as chairperson of the Uttar Pradesh Film Devlopment Board. She was made a scapegoat for no reason. Fortunately she was renominated as Member of Parliament, Rajya Sabha in June 2006.

* * *

John Abraham

John Abraham was born on 17 December 1972 in Bombay. He began earning as a media planner while working with an ad agency. One of his clients was the Cadila company for which Bipasha Basu used to model. He would plan beautiful Bipasha Basu's advertising campaigns. Being in the media world, he was signed for the film 'Aitbaar' in 2004 with Bipasha Basu as the heroine. But it was Mahesh Bhatt's 'Jism' that brought him into limelight. Both Bipasha and John acted together in this film which helped to establish him as an actor though Bipasha was already a star at that time. She helped him a lot in the film. Inspired at the success of this film, he was signed by different filmmakers. During the year 2004, he worked with Bipasha Basu in 'Aitbaar' and 'Madhosh', with the latter proving a complete disaster. The second film of his career, 'Saaya' with actress Tara Sharma, was an action-packed film. Director Pooja Bhatt's film 'Paap' in 2003 opposite Udita Goswami earned him much praise and this film was also screened at a film festival in Pakistan.

John is very friendly with Abhishek Bachchan and he enjoyed working with him and Esha Deol in 'Dhoom' in 2004 and the film became a successful hit. He played the lead role in 'Elaan' in 2005 opposite Lara Dutta and the film had plenty of daring bike-riding shots. He did with all seriousness his role in 'Karam' in 2005 opposite Priyanka Chopra but the film did not do well. His career got a boost when he acted with Amitabh Bachchan in 'Viruddh', in Ajay Devgan's 'Kaal' and in 'Shikhar' with Lara Dutta and Bipasha Bsasu. He worked in 'Garam Masala' with Akshay Kumar and this proved a great training ground for him. He boldly performed a negative role in 'Zinda' with veteran actor Sanjay Dutt and heroine Lara Dutta. He did playback singing too for this film.

He is drawing attention of filmmakers and has signed a number of new ventures yet to be released. John's latest film 'Taxi Number 9 2 11' became a hit film. During the shooting of a film at Kabul, his body clock stopped. He had to be rushed back and admitted to a hospital in Mumbai.

* * *

Juhi Chawla

Juhi Chawa, a veteran actress, smiles with her bewitching black eyes and is five feet four inches tall. Born on 13 November 1967 at Ludhiana, Punjab, she joined the glamour world while modelling. She won the Miss India crown as well as the Best Costumes Award in the Miss Universe contest in 1984. Producer Arjun Hingorani's film '*Sultanat*' in 1986 was her debut film with debutant Karan Kapoor, who also came from the field of modelling. The film did not do well but she was accepted and she continued to grow with every role that she performed. She acted in producer Nasir Husain's film '*Qayamat se Qayamat Tak*' in 1988 opposite Aamir Khan. This film was a super hit.

Gradually every filmmaker wanted to cast her in his film as she was the hot star of Bollywood then. Producer B. Shubhash cast her with Aamir Khan in his film '*Love Love Love*' in 1989 but it flopped. Director Yash Chopra made her give a guest appearance in his multi-starrer film '*Chandni*' in 1989. It was a hit film. She also played in '*Vicky Dada*', a dubbed film. She performed a good role in Jalal Agha's film '*Goonj*' opposite Kumar Gaurav. During this period she performed in a good number of films including a non-Hindi film, '*Nattukku Oru Nallavan*' in 1991. A good chemistry developed between Shah Rukh Khan and her when she worked with him in '*Raju Ban Gaya Gentleman*' in 1992. It was a rollicking comedy.

Juhi rode on the path of success with one hit film after another. She acted with Govinda in '*Radha ka Sangam*' and with Rishi Kapoor in '*Bol Radha Bol*' in 1992. Her image improved greatly with Dharmesh Darshan's '*Lootere*' in 1993 opposite Sunny Deol. Her most successful film was Yash Chopra's '*Darr*' in 1993 opposite Shah Rukh Khan. The film became a super hit. Director Mukesh Bhatt's film '*Hum Hain Rahi Pyaar Ke*' in 1993 and '*Duplicate*' in 1998 with Shah Rukh Khan helped her to gain popularity. She won the Filmfare Award for Best Actress for '*Hum Hain Rahi Pyaar Ke*' and NY Bollywood Award in 1999 for the Most Sensational Performance in '*Duplicate*'.

Hrishikesh Mukherjee's film '*Jhooth Bole Kauwwa Kaate*' in 1998 with her and Anil Kapoor became memorable due to her qualitative performance. Her role in the historical film '*Shaheed Udham Singh*' in 2000 was critically acclaimed. Her other memorable films have been '*Eena Meena Deeka*', '*Phir Bhi Dil Hai Hindustani*', '*Yes Boss*', '*Aamdani Atthanni Kharcha Rupaiya*', '*Jhankaar Beats*' and '*Paheli*' in 2005. She has a good number of films in her kitty yet to be released.

Juhi Chawla founded a production company with Shah Rukh Khan and called it Dreamz Unlimited under which she produced '*Phir Bhi Dil Hai Hindustani*' in 2000 and '*Chalte Chalte*' in 2003 by acting opposite Shah Rukh Khan. Under the banner of Archlight and Films Pvt Ltd, she co-produced the period film '*Asoka*' in 2001 with Kareena Kapoor. Her ambitious film '*Paheli*' with Shah Rukh Khan and Rani Mukherjee was nominated for the Oscar Award. It was a rare honour for her.

Juhi is happily married to businessman Jai Mehta and lives with him and their two children. She has nearly stopped acting in films.

* * *

Kajol

Kajol was born on 5 August 1975 and hails from a family of film celebrities. Her father Shomu Mukerjee was a producer and mother Tanuja has been an actress of yester years. Her grandmother Shobhana Samarth and aunt Nutan were established actresses of their time. Her younger sister Tanisha has also started her career in films. Kajol's debut film was Rahul Rawail's 'Bekhudi' in 1992 opposite Kamal Sadhana. It was a flop film but her performance in 'Yeh Dillagi' in 1994 opposite Akshay Kumar established her as a promising actress. She is a natural and spontaneous performer. She does not like nor believe in hypocrisy for she is a straightforward person. She took to this profession as a hobby. She has never compromised on her career for the sake of money. She has a good number of hits to her credit and she is an optimist at heart.

Kajol got married to actor Ajay Devgan at the peak of her career to settle down to married life. On 20 April 2003, she gave birth to a daughter and named her Nysa after a Greek goddess. In between she became the brand ambassador for a jewellery designing firm and has modelled for Samsung products. After a successful stint in the modelling field with her husband Ajay Devgan, she has started helping him with Ajay Devgan Production Company engaged in distribution of films. Her memorable films have been Guddu Dhanoa's 'Goondaraj', director Anees Bazmee's 'Hulchul' in 1995, Indra Kumar's 'Ishq' in 1997 and 'Pyaar to Hona Hi Tha' in 1998 and in all these films she acted with Ajay Devgan.

She kept away from the arc lights of the silver screen for some time to take care of her daughter Nysa but now she has again returned to the film world. Her latest film 'Fanaa' released in May 2006 opposite Aamir Khan and Abhishek Bachchan has once again proved what a talented actress she is. She now wants to work in one or two select films at a time.

Kajol has performed with superstar Shah Rukh Khan in a number of hit films like Rakesh Roshan's 'Karan Arjun', Abbas Mastan's 'Bazigar' in 1993, Karan Johar's 'Kuch Kuch Hota Hai' in 1998, 'Dil Wale Dulhaniya Le Jayenge' in 1995 (a super hit film), and 'Kabhi Khushi Kabhi Gham' in 2001. The last named film was a blockbuster. Her other important films have been 'Gupt' with Bobby Deol, 'Hameshaa' with Saif Ali Khan and 'Dushman' with Sanjay Dutt.

Kajol is still energetic, enthusiastic and ready to honour any commitment she may make to the film world.

* * *

Kareena Kapoor

Kareena Kapoor is the grand daughter of the great showman, the late Raj Kapoor and is only twenty-five years old. Nick-named Bebo, she hails from the family of one of the oldest in the film world. She is the daughter of Babita who was a well-known actress of her time and of father Randhir Kapoor who is an actor-director-producer. Karishma Kapoor, her elder sister, is a well-known heroine and is married and settled in Delhi. Kareena is five feet five inches tall with a peaches-and-cream complexion. Her blue eyes can mesmerise anyone and she is a total extrovert. She briefly attended the Government Law College after graduating from Cathedral School. Initially she wanted to join Harvard but destiny had ordained that she join the film industry.

Sources in the film world claim that Kareena's launch into Bollywood was delayed so that her sister Karishma could get a head start. There is no denying that the two sisters dote on each other and Kareena is reported to have said, "We're always looking out for each other. We're sisters first and everything else later." Even as a ten-year elder, Kareena used to try on wigs and new shades of lipsticks, etc. in her sister's make-up room and everyone had presumed that she too would join the film industry and that too make for a successful career. Even her mother Babita, who rules with an iron hand both her daughters, could not foretell that her daughter would reach such heights as an actress.

Kareena's dramatic entrance into the film world with her debut in J.P. Dutta's 'Refugee' in 2001 against Abhishek Bachchan did not create any waves and the film was mediocre, but she had expected it to be a super hit. In this film she performed the role of a simple village girl. With her flawless and translucent skin she managed to carve out a niche for herself as a performing actress and not a mere glamorous doll. Her film 'Asoka' with Shah Rukh Khan, 'Yaadein' and 'Main Prem ki Deewani Hun' bombed at the box-office. Her early film career was not a successful one. But with the box-office success of her films like 'Mujhe Kuch Kahna Hai' and 'Kabhi Khushi Kabhi Gham' with Shah Rukh and Hrithik Roshan have ranked her as a good actress.

Her face is innocent and her acting is natural and without inhibitions. She is professionally a mature actress. Today she is one of the best saleable heroines of Bollywood. She is charming and glamorous. She wanted to become a movie star since childhood.

During the year 2003, she did not leave any impact on the filmdom, though she remained in the news round the year. She had high expectations from Rajshri's film 'Main Prem ki Deewani Hun' but this film was mediocre. Films like 'Khushi' and 'Talaash' also met with the same fate. Although from Director J.P. Dutta's film 'LoC-Kargil' in 2003 she had very high expectations for its success, the film did not do well despite her acting with all seriousness. Her exemplary role in Sudhir Mishra's film 'Chameli' in 2004 successfully proved her to be a talented actress. It was based on the life of a call-girl and she revealed her talent by performing this artistic role. She received the Stardust Special Award for her performance in 'Chameli'.

Mani Ratnam's film 'Yuva' was a normal film. In Govind Nihalani's film 'Dev' she acted a Muslim

woman. *'Fida'* in 2004 with Shahid Kapoor and Fardeen Khan proved a flop film. It did not do even average business. Her performance in *'Fida'* was appreciated in every corner, however. *'Aitraaz'* in 2004 by Abbas Mastan and with Akshay Kumar too was an average masala film. Doe-eyed Kareena's *'Hulchul'* in 2004 with Akshaye Khanna was a box-office hit. Boney Kapoor's film *'Bewafaa'* in 2005 starring Anil Kapoor and Akshay Kumar was mediocre.

During her short career in Bollywood, she has worked in many films and received appreciation. She worked in *'Jeena Sirf Mere Liye'* in 2002, *'Talaash'* and *'The Hunt Begins'* in 2003, *'Kyon Ki'* and successful *'Dosti'* with Akshay Kumar in 2005. At present she has no plans to marry but wants to concentrate seriously on her career and act in films of directors of repute.

* * *

Karishma Kapoor

Karishma Kapoor alias Lolo, daughter of producer-director-actor Randhir Kapoor and former film star Babita, is also the great grand daughter of veteran Prithviraj Kaoor and grand daughter of the great showman, Raj Kapoor. Her younger sister Kareena Kapoor has become an established name in the film world after working for the first time as an actress in J.P. Dutta's film *'Refugee'*.

Karishma made her debut in *'Prem Qaidi'* in 1991 when she was barely sixteen-years old. Her mother Babita is a very ambitious lady and she started looking for a chance to give her daughter a break in films while she was still in Cathedral School. Though her first film was *'Danga Fasaad'* in 1990, the film bombed miserably. She worked with different filmmakers but none could establish her in Bollywood, till she was paired with Govinda in *'Raja Babu'*, *'Khuddar'*, *'Coolie No. 1'*, *'Saajan Chale Sasural'* and *'Hero No.1'*. She became glamorous and hot among the stars in the industry and among the masses by performing dance numbers on songs like *'Sexy, sexy mujhe log bole& '* in *'Khuddar'* and *'Sarkailey khatiya& '* in *'Raja Babu'*. She became a superstar with *'Raja Hindustani'* in 1996 where she gave intimate kiss scenes with Aamir Khan. The film proved commercially successful and marked a turning point in her career. She won the Filmfare Award for Best Actress in 1996 for this film. Her performance in *'Dil to Paagal Hai'* was most competitive as she was pitted against Madhuri Dixit, the most popular actress of her time. She performed a vigorous dance number which she had never presented before. She won the National Film Award for Best Supporting Actress and the Filmfare Award for the film. One after another her films like *'Haseena Maan Jaayegi'*, *'Biwi No.1'*, *'Hum Saath Saath Hain'* and *'Janwar'* became hits. Her career graph began to rise with every film and so did her looks and confidence.

In 2002, she got the chance to prove her acting ability in a serious film, *'Fiza'* with Jaya Bachchan and she played a brilliant role as a terrorist's sister. She won the Filmfare Award for Best Actress for her role which was critically acclaimed. She played the title role in Shyam Benegal's *'Zubeida'* as second wife to a prince. The film won her the second National Film Award for Best Actress. Her role in Boney Kapoor's film *'Shakti'* proved her to be an actress of elegance. She performed commendably in a TV serial *'Karishma   A Miracle of Destiny'*. Her other memorable films are *'Jigar'*, *'Deedar'*, *'Anari'*, *'Andaaz'*, *'Dulaara'*, *'Jawab'*, *'Mrityudaata'*, *'Baaz   A Bird in Danger'* in 2005.

Meanwhile her father Randhir Kapoor had to undergo heart surgery in Delhi and this made her cancel her shooting and attend to her father. After a log courtship and engagement to Abhishek Bachchan, she got married instead to her childhood friend Sanjay Kapoor, a Delhi-based businessman, on 29 September 2003. She gave birth to daughter Samaira, a beautiful child though her marriage was going through a bad phase. In July 2005, she started divorce proceedings against her husband Sanjay, but later they reconciled in court. They even went to Goa for their second wedding anniversary and sorted out their differences. Today she is leading a happy married life with her husband.

* * *

K. L. Saigal

K. L. Saigal

Kundan Lal Saigal, the legendary singing superstar of the early thirties, became famous for his acting prowess and tuneful popular songs in some very memorable films. His aura and charisma still remains intact. Long before actors Shah Rukh Khan or Amitabh Bachchan appeared on the scene, Saigal with his sober and pathetic voice continued to haunt the masses. Such was his mystique and acceptance by the masses that playback singers like Mukesh and Kishore Kumar started their career by imitating his singing style that became famous as the 'Saigal style'. He became the first male superstar of Hindi cinema and created the grammar of film singing in the nascent Indian talkie era.

Born on 4 April 1904 in Jammu, he was the son of Amar Chand Saigal who was a *tehsildar* in the court of Maharaja Pratap Singh of Jammu & Kashmir. His mother Kesar Bai was a religious lady, who was fond of music. She used to take him to *bhajan*, *keertan* and *shabad* functions and at times to a Sufi saint, Pir Salman Yousuf of Yesvi sect. At the age of thirteen, Saigal realised that his voice was cracking and this so shocked him that he remained silent for a couple of months. His worried parents were advised by the saint to make him practice and cultivate his voice. He did as advised single-mindedly for three years, due to which, he was able to attain a difference in the tone and texture of notes. At the age of twelve, Saigal gave a rendition of Meera's *bhajan* in Pratap Singh's court. The Maharaja was so impressed that he predicted that Saigal had a bright singing future. In Jalandhar, Saigal learnt to sing in the Punjabi style. Surprisingly he did not undergo any formal training in music. Later on in life, he learnt the finer nuances of music from the great masters of the period: Faiyaaz Khan, Pankaj Mullick and Pahari Sanyal.

His formal schooling was brief and uneventful. His father was absolutely against his singing and was disappointed with his poor results at school. So Saigal left home and reached Calcutta. Before choosing music and singing as his vocation, he worked as a time-keeper in the Punjab Railways. He was a salesman for a short while, selling typewriters. In those days, his singing was largely confined to the friend circle. At one such private concert, a sales representative of the Hindustan Record Company, Rai Chand Boral, was present. He immediately recognised Saigal's talent and the sales potential of his records if he were to be signed up for the recording company. Saigal was persuaded to enter into a lifetime contract with this company and one of his early records, 'Jhulana jhulao& ' in raga Deva Gandhar became an instant hit.

In 1932, Kundan Lal Saigal's successful career commenced after he signed a contract of 200 rupees per month with New Theatres to act and sing in films. Some of the films in his early days were 'Subah ka Sitare', 'Zinda Laash' and 'Mohabbat ke Aasoon'. The first two did not do well and the last named starring heroine Akhtari Moradabadi was based on a drama called 'Zehr-e-Ishq' and in which Saigal was given a very small role. However his song 'Radhe Raini de daaro na bansari mori re& ' from the film 'Pooran Bhagat' in 1933 created a sensation throughout India. His brilliant singing style established him as a good singer. He worked in 'Rajrani Meera' and 'Yahudi ki Ladki' in 1933 but it was by working in 'Chandidas' in 1934 that he attained stardom. It was his first successful film wherein he played the role of an idealist poet, worshipper, lover of humanity and priest of a temple. Songs like 'Premnagar mein basaoongi ghar main& ', 'Tadapat beeti din rain& ' and 'Prem ki ho jai& ' from this film in which Saigal was the lead actor, catapulted him to great

heights. He did around 20 films for producer B.N. Sircar in the first phase up to 1940, some of them being 'Devdas' in 1935, 'Crorepati' in 1936, 'Zindagi' in 1940 and 'Lagan' in 1941. The real breakthrough for him came in 1935 with the film 'Devdas' which was based on the famous novel of Sarat Chandra Chattopadhyay and in which Saigal played the role of Devdas, the son of an affluent zamindar. He rendered all-time favourite songs like 'Balam aaye baso morey man mein& ' This film established him as the first superstar of Hindi cinema. It created history and continues to haunt moviegoers even today when technology has advanced such a lot.

His films 'President' and 'Street Singer' were other milestones in his career. He acted as a mill-worker and sang the most memorable song of his time: 'Ik bangla bane nyaaraa& ' in 'President' and performed the unbelievable role of a street singer who sang on roads immortal songs like 'Babul mora naihar chhooto hee jaaye& '. These songs still haunt the masses and attained wide popularity during his days. He also sang some other unforgettable songs.

Saigal also acted in several Bengali films produced by New Theatres and sang about 50 Bengali songs. He was conversant with Bengali too. He left New Theatres, Calcutta and reached Bombay in December 1940.

At Bombay he joined Ranjit Movietone in 1941 and acted in this company's 'Bhakt Surdas' in 1942, 'Tansen' in 1943 and 'Bhanwara' in 1944. He did for New Theatres the film 'Meri Behan' in 1944 and sang another immortal song: 'Aye qatib-e-taqdeer mujhe itna bataa de& '. Director-producer A.R. Kardar's historical film, 'Shahjahan' in 1946, was one of the most successful, memorable and melodious films of Saigal. He rendered his best songs at the fag end of his life: 'Gham diye mustaqil& ', 'Kar leejiye chal kar meri jannat ka nazaara& ', 'Jab dil hee toot gayaa& ', 'Aye dil-e-beqaraar jhoom& ', 'Chah barbaad kareggee hamein maloom na tha& '. From 1932 to 1946, the Hindi film world was called as 'K.L. Saigal musical era'.

Saigal acted in about 29 Hindi films and sang about 150 film songs and about 100 non-film songs. The range of his songs was vast   he sang *khayal*, *bandish*, *ghazal*, *geet*, *bhajan*, *hori* and *dadra* in numerous *ragas*. He sang in Hindi, Urdu, Pushto, Punjabi, Bengali and Tamil languages. His distinct voice transcended Saigal the actor. He could render light classical songs with utmost ease. His style was such that he normally sang in lower octaves, which was emulated by many but was unmatched. It was said that he never recorded without drinking (he used to call a peg, Kali Paanch).

Some believe that Saigal had a premonition about his death and that was the reason why he quickly completed the shooting of his last film. He died before the country could gain Independence at Jalandhar at 6.00 a.m. on 18 January 1947, at the age of forty-two depriving music lovers of his ethereal voice.

Saigal had one son Madan and two daughters, Nina and Bina. None of his children are now alive and his younger daughter Bina Chopra left this world in October 2001 in Delhi. Saigal's last film 'Parwana' was released after his death on 9 May 1947. Fifty years since his demise, Saigal still lingers in the memories of music lovers as an immortal singer.

* * *

Lata Mangeshkar

Lata Mangeshkar

Lata Mangeshkar, the 'Melody Queen' of India, is one of her kind in the world of music and cinema. She does not need any introduction. Songs rendered by her are most popular throughout the world and she has become a universal icon. She was a nominated member of Rajya Sabha.

Born in 1929 at Indore, she was named Hema, then Latika while her surname was changed from Hardikar to Mangeshkar. She rendered a heartfelt song 'Ae mere watan ke logon& ' on 27 January 1963 as a tribute to the martyrs who lost their lives in the war with China.

Her father was Dinanath Mangeshkar, who was a classical singer and stage actor. Initially she was not allowed to sing for films even. It was around March 1942 that her father granted her permission to sing only one song in the Marathi film 'Kiti Hsaal' in 1942 but sadly enough, it was not used. He was even against girls acting on the stage or in films. Unfortunately her father died when she was only thirteen-years old. She being the eldest had to take the responsibility of the well-being of her siblings. She acted in her debut film 'Pehli Mangalagaur' in 1942 performing the role of the heroine's younger sister. Basically she was never interested to act but she had no alternative. She preferred singing to acting. Her first love was anyway singing. She was conferred the Padma Bhushan in 1969, the Dada Saheb Phalke Award in 1989, the Filmfare Awards for 'Madhumati', 'Bees Saal Baad', 'Khandaan', 'Jeene ki Raah' in 1969. She renounced the Filmfare Awards after 1969 saying that these be given in future to new upcoming singers. The Bharat Ratna, India's highest civilian honour, was bestowed on her in 2001.

She acted in Marathi films like 'Chimukala Sansaar' in 1943, 'Mazee Bal' in 1943, 'Gajabhau ' in 1944, and in Hindi films like 'Badi Maa' in 1945, 'Jeevan Yatra' in 1946, 'Subhadra' in 1946, 'Mandir' in 1948 and 'Chhatrapati Shivaji' in 1952. She composed music for Marathi films like 'Ramram Paahune' in 1950, 'Mohityanchi Manjula' in 1962, 'Maratha Tituka Melvava' in 1964, 'Saadhi Manse' in 1965 and 'Taambadi Maati' in 1969. She produced films such as 'Vaadal' in Marathi in 1953 and in Hindi, films like 'Kanchan' in 1955, 'Lekin' in 1988, and 'Jhaanjhar' in 1953 with C. Ramachandran.

At first she rendered two songs in Vasant Joglekar's film 'Aapki Sewa Mein' in 1947. She sang for the first time under the direction of musician Harishchander Baali. She also sang for C. Ramachander's 'Shehnai' and rendered her first song for Ghulam Haider's film 'Majboor' in 1948 --- 'Dil mera toda mujhe kanhi ka na chhoda& ' Mukesh also sang one song with her --- 'Ab darne ki baat nahin angreji chhora chala gaya& ' Her first song for Naushad was in 'Chandni Raat'. During this period, she sang songs for 'Lahore', 'Dulari', 'Andaz', 'Bazaar', 'Ziddi' and 'Aasha'. All the songs of the film 'Andaz' became most popular, particularly 'Chup chup khade ho zaroor koi baat hai& ' of 'Badi Behan' and which was composed by Husanlal Bhagatram. Her songs of 'Barsaat' composed by debutant music maestro Shanker and Jaikishen were heard throughout the country. 'School Girl' was the first film with Anil Biswas and with the super success of 'Andaz' and 'Barsaat' she became the topmost singing star of India. Her melodious voice reached its zenith with the success of her film 'Mahal'. She has created history in singing; the rest is history.

Lata Mangeshkar has three younger sisters, namely Meena Khadilkar, Asha Bhosle, Usha Mangeshkar and a musician brother Hridaynath Mangeshkar. She, with the help of her family members, has constructed a hospital in memory of her father which was opened to the public on 5 December 2001. She is not only a singing star but above all, a kind and lovable human being.

* * *

Madhubala

Madhubala

Inarguably the most beautiful artiste to ever grace the Indian screen, Madhubala was given the title 'Venus of the Indian Screen' by Baburao Patel, editor of *Filmindia* magazine published some thirty years ago. Beginning from a most humble life, she rose to become the most captivating star India has ever produced. She was the most beautiful and glamorous heroine ever seen in Bollywood. She was vivacious, sensuous and possessed a million-watt smile that captivated anyone who saw or met her.

Born as Begum Mumtaz Jehan on 14 February 1933, which happened to be Valentine's Day, she came from a poor and conservative family of Muslim Pathans. Her father Ataullah Khan used to live in a *jhopda* near Bombay Talkies Studio in Malad, Bombay. When her father lost his job with the Indian Tobacco Company, she was only eight-years old. She was the third of six daughters and the most beautiful among them. He took her to Bombay Talkies and got her an audition. She was selected as a child artiste and called Baby Mumtaz for the film '*Basant*' made in 1942, starring Mumtaz Shanti and Ulhas. With the success of her role in this first film of hers, she was engaged in films by other filmmakers and she acted in '*Mumtaz Mahal*' in 1944, '*Dhanna Bhagat*' and '*Pujari*' in 1945. She was well appreciated and soon became the heart-throb of millions of people and film directors.

Director Kidar Sharma was looking for a new face in the debut film of Raj Kapoor. He spotted the thirteen-year old Baby Mumtaz and signed her as the heroine of his film '*Neel Kamal*' in 1947. It happened to be a debut film as heroine for Madhubala too. Mumtaz was renamed Madhubala by Devika Rani, the First Lady of Indian Cinema. The word 'Madhubala' means a 'damsel of honey'.

Within a span of three years up to 1950, she gave brilliant performances in about twenty-four films with different directors and heroes and films like '*Chittor Vijay*', '*Dil ki Rani*', '*Amar Prem*', '*Lal Dupatta*', '*Dulari*,' etc. brought her fame and name. She became the most talked about star in the country after working in Bombay Talkies' film '*Mahal*' by acting with Ashok Kumar. Her beauty was a million times better presented on the screen. She became the most successful heroine of the Indian cinema with the success of this film. She acted as a gardener's daughter and haunted the hero with her melodious song '*Ayega aanewala&* '. This was one of the best songs ever sung by Lata Mangeshkar.

As it is said that her beauty overshadowed her acting talents, it proved true to an extent in her case too; however this was more due to her poor judgement than lack of talent. Being encumbered by a large family to support and forever living under the domination of her father, she made several poor choices in movies that seriously undermined her credibility as a serious performer, to the extent of being labelled '*box-office poison*'. However, her more or less dismal repertoire in the fifties was marked by spots of brilliance with movies like '*Tarana*' in 1951, '*Mr & Mrs 55*' in 1955 and of course, her swansong '*Mughal-e-Azam*' in 1960 which showcased her remarkable talents as a serious artiste across several genres and revealed what this ethereal beauty was truly capable of.

The film 'Mughal-e-Azam' took ten long years in its making. It is one of the milestones in Indian cinema and a successful historical film. The film in its totality had superb performances put in by Prithviraj Kapoor, Dilip Kumar, Durga Khote and Nigar Sultana. The magnitude of its canvass with splendid performances by the aritstes took the film to a super box-office success. With this film Madhubala reached the zenith of her career. The dance sequence in the Sheesh Mahal as Anarkali by her acting on the song 'Jab pyaar kiya to darna kya& ' has become immortal in Lata Mangeshkar's voice. This film was screened in 2006 in Pakistan for the first time after a gap of about forty years with the ban imposed on screening of Hindi films there.

During the making of her film 'Chalti ka Naam Gaadi' in 1958, Madhubala was drawn towards singer-actor Kishore Kumar and she ultimately got married to him. They worked in 'Mehlon ke Khwab' in 1960, 'Jhumroo' in 1961 and 'Half-ticket' in 1962. It is said that she received marriage proposals from Bharat Bhushan, Pradeep Kumar, Shammi Kapoor and Kishore Kumar. But she chose Kishore Kumar, who got converted to Islam to marry her.

Madhubala's best films before her death were 'Barsaat ki Raat' with Bharat Bhushan, 'Jaali Note' in 1960 and 'Sharabi' in 1964 with Dev Anand. She was one of the most versatile actresses of her time. She worked in about seventy films in her film career. She was suffering with a congenital heart problem. After she was diagnosed as having a hole in her heart, she put up a brave front and her illness was kept a secret from the industry for many years. She frequently coughed out blood on the sets and was confined to bed for about nine tortuous years. Eventually her illness forced her to end her career.

She used to say that God had been good to her and it was for her to be good to others. Her last film 'Jwala' in 1971 with Sunil Dutt was released after her death. She died on 23 February 1969, nine days after her thirty-sixth birthday in despair, grief and with a broken heart. To this day she remains one of the most enduring legends of Indian cinema.

* * *

Madhuri Dixit

Madhuri Dixit nee Madhuri Nene was one of the most popular actresses of the 1990s. Her charismatic smile reaching her eyes floored the masses. She hails from a middle-class Maharashtrian family and is the fifth child of her businessman father. Her mother had completed her post-graduation in music after marriage. She even took lessons from her mother in music. She is a trained classical dancer and wanted to be a microbiologist.

Madhuri made her debut in Rajshri Production's film 'Abodh' in 1984 but the film was rejected by the audience as well as by the industry. She was taken in second lead roles in 'Awara Baap' in 1985 and 'Swati' in 1986. These films did not help her in establishing herself. In the competitive market of filmdom, director Subhash Ghai introduced her as a lead heroine in his film 'Uttar Dakshin' in 1987 but it too bombed at the box-office. But her godfather, Subhash Ghai did not give up and reintroduced her in 'Ram Lakhan' in 1988 while N. Chandra signed her for his next film 'Tejaab'. She worked with all seriousness in these films. Her films now began to reveal Madhuri's beauty and people dubbed her as the reincarnation of the erstwhile Madhubala, the Venus of Hindi Cinema. Madhuri became a star with the hugely successful hit number 'Ek do teen& ' from the film and it took the nation by storm. She became a name to be reckoned with overnight with her hit films. It was her first step towards stardom. Subsequently her performance in 'Dil' in 1990 was superb and so was it as a quarrelling daughter-in-law in the film 'Beta' in 1992 with Anil Kapoor. It was a remake of the Telugu film 'Enga Chinna Rasa'. She won her first Filmfare Award for Best Actress for her role in 'Beta' and became the top heroine of Bollywood with her dance numbers on songs like 'Dhak dhak& ' and 'Choli ke peeche kya hai& ' from 'Khalnayak' in 1993 and which were choreographed by Saroj Khan. Her magnetic dance movements became commercially viable for the filmmakers. Items with a liberal dose of jhatkas not only propelled her towards stardom but also established Saroj Khan as a hot dance-director. On the flip side, it was this song of 'Khalnayak' that caused a stir, with women's liberation groups asking for a ban on Madhuri. She played the role of a policewoman in this film.

In the film 'Anjaan' in 1994, she played the role of an avenging angel. In the year 1994, she enacted the role of a very charming and mischievous daughter-in-law in 'Hum Aapke Hain Kaun' in 1994, which became a blockbuster, grossing a huge amount of money that any Hindi film had ever done. With this film she reached the zenith of her career. She won another Filmfare Award for Best Actress for this film. Her popularity ensured the success of 'Raja' in 1995 and Madhuri became the 'female Amitabh Bachchan' with her all-round versatility.

After the success of 'Raja', for some time her career graph dipped and her films such as 'Prem Diwani', 'Phool', 'Sahiban', 'Prem Pooja', 'Anjaam', 'Yaarana', 'Prem Granth', 'Rajkumar', and 'Mohabbat' failed to leave behind any impact. While she was worried at her troubled career, producer-director Yash Chopra gave her boost in his film 'Dil to Pagal Hai' in 1997. It was a phenomenal success at the box-office, with her finding mass acceptance from the audience. Madhuri never looked better, danced better or acted better; this film of hers was indeed her best till date. Madhuri went on to win a handful of awards for her performance in 'Dil to Pagal Hai', and

even dedicated her Filmfare Award to her critics. In 1998, Madhuri had only one major film to her credit and that was C.N. Chandra's *Wajood*. Unfortunately the film failed to recreate the hysteria of *Tejaab* of 1998. An off-beat film of director Prakash Jha's, *Mrityudand*, proved her a talented and serious actor. It ensured critical acclaim if not box-office success for her. Madhuri still had the fire that was shown in *Tejaab* and the intensity that came to light in *Beta*. She played five different roles in renowned painter M.F. Husain's film *Gajagamini* in 2002. The media had by now written her obituary and announced that it was time for her to pack her bags and get married. Madhuri co-starring with Akshaye Khanna, who was younger in age to her in *Mohabbat*, was criticised by one and all. She acted in *Koyla* and director Rakesh Roshan stated that Madhuri could no longer play the role of a young girl but her response was a dignified silence. After a short gap she gave a splendid performance in *Pukar* and subsequently in *Lajja* where her super performance bagged for her the Best Supporting Actor Award in the Lux Zee Cine Awards for 2002.

She got married during the making of other films to US-based cardio-thoracic surgeon Dr Shriram Nene, who is permanently settled in the US. After marriage she did not quit films and did only two films *Devdas* and K.C. Bokadia's film *Hum Tumhare Hain Sanam*. Her priorities towards family, society and Bollywood have changed now. She has two kids (Arin and Ryan) and her parents are also settled in the USA. She gave a live performance of nine minutes on the stage at the Filmfare Awards function in March 2006 during her visit to Mumbai after a gap of four years. Today she has no regrets about leaving the film industry. If she were to stage a comeback, the industry would welcome her with open arms.

* * *

Meena Kumari

The 'tragedy queen' of Bollywood was none other than Meena Kumari. She was the daughter of a Hindu-Muslim marriage and was born on 1 August 1932 in Bombay. Her father was an actor with the Parsi Theatre. The harmonium-playing Master Alibux came to Bombay leaving behind his wife and three daughters to become a musician. He got married to Prabhavati the second time when she used to work in silent films. After marriage Prabhavati changed her name to' Iqbal Begum. Mahajabeen alias Meena Kumari was their second child. She used to play in the courtyard of Rooptara Studios just opposite her house. Director Vijay Bhatt introduced her at the age of six as Baby Meena, in the role of a child artiste in '*Leatherface*' in 1939. She led a life of struggle in this profession. When it was time for her to play with dolls, she herself became a doll for others. Her father had little or no source of income. She played the leading role of heroine Gauri in Vijay Bhatt's musical film '*Baiju Bawra*' in 1952. It was a big hit and for this film, Baby Meena was renamed Meena Kumari. With the success of this film she became a star. She won the first Filmfare Award for Best Actress in 1953 for '*Baiju Bawra*'.

Meena Kumari was sober, emotional and fond of *ghazals*. During this period, she was deeply drawn towards director Kamaal Amrohi and ultimately got married to him in 1953. But her married life was never easy. She severed her relations with her husband in 1964. Her anguish-filled voice attracted the masses. She was the main earning member of her large family. Prior to '*Baiju Bawra*', she had performed in social and mythological films like '*Veer Ghatotkach*', '*Shree Ganesh Mahima*', '*Hanuman*', '*Pataal*', '*Vijay*' and '*Lakshmi Narayan*' in 1951.

Ashok Kumar produced '*Parineeta*' in 1953 with himself acting as the hero opposite Meena Kumari. The film was directed by Bimal Roy and proved to be a big hit. She won the Filmfare Award for Best Actress for this film. Her portrayal as a grief-stricken woman earned her name and fame. She used to perform her roles from the core of her heart. Her life was never comfortable or smooth. Director B.R. Chopra's '*Ek hi Raasta*' in 1956 was based on a typical social theme. She acted brilliantly and won acclaim. Her performance in director L.V. Prasad's film '*Sharada*' in 1957 with Raj Kapoor as her lover who becomes her stepson was superb. After working in '*Dil Apna aur Preet Parayi*' in 1960, her life took a new turn.

Meena Kumari used to play lighthearted roles in films to comfort herself as seen in '*Naya Andaaz*', '*Azad*', '*Naulakha Haaar*', '*Ilzaam*', '*Miss Mary*' and '*Shararat*', etc. Her performance in Guru Dutt's '*Sahib Bibi aur Ghulam*' in 1962 as Chhoti Bahu was critically acclaimed by one and all. She won the Filmfare Award as Best Actress for '*Sahib Bibi aur Ghulam*'. Her films '*Dil Ek Mandir*', '*Kajal*' and '*Phool aur Patthar*' cemented her image further as a successful heroine. During the period of her estrangement from her husband, she was drawn towards Dharmendra and later to Gulzar. She won another Filmfare Award for '*Kajal*' in 1965. Her most memorable film was producer-director Kamaal Amrohi's '*Pakeezah*' whose shooting was started in 1963 but completed only in 1971. The melodious music and lyrics of this film became popular hits of the period. It became the most successful film after her death and is considered a landmark in Indian films' history.

She performed character roles in 'Jawaab' and 'Dushman', etc. She even played the role of an old woman in Gulzar's directorial debut and producer R.N. Sippy's film 'Mer Apne' in 1970. It was a tragic role. Her other memorable films were 'Aarti', 'Main Chup Rahungi', 'Chitralekha', 'Bahu Begum', 'Footpath', 'Yahudi', 'Kohinoor', 'Ghazal', 'Noorjehan', etc.

The last days of her life were passed in anonymity and solitude. She was heart-broken as she had reposed faith in all the wrong persons who let her down. She took to heavy drinking of alcohol. During this period she stayed either at home or in hospital, composing *ghazals* which were published by Gulzar after her death. She died on 31 March 1972 from cirrhosis of liver and after a few weeks of the release of her film *'Pakeezah'*. She died a sad death while struggling for life in hospital due to lack of financial assistance from her relations, who had drained her earnings during her heydays.

* * *

Nargis

Nargis was one of the most successful stars after Independence. She was soft-spoken, sweet-natured and unconventional. Her personality and glamorous looks attracted one and all. She was known as the 'lady in white', as she took to wearing only white clothes after her association with the legendary Raj Kapoor. She was a unique artiste amongst all the actresses and as beautiful as the flower known as 'nargis'.

She was born in Calcutta on 1 June 1929 as Fatima Rashid. Her mother Jaddan Bai was an actress, singer, music composer and filmmaker. She was a Muslim from Punjab but grew up in Allahabad. Nargis's father Uttamchand Mohanchand alias Mohan Babu, was a Mahiyal Brahmin from Rawalpindi, Punjab and had studied medicine to become a doctor. But after meeting Jaddan bai, his life changed. They got married in Calcutta in 1928. Jaddan Bai was twenty-seven years old, with two sons — the elder Akhtar Hussain and the younger Anwar Hussain — from her first marriage. The family shifted to Bombay in late 1934. Nargis joined the Queen Mary's High School and after passing Senior Cambridge, she did not join any college. She was not drawn towards bioscope (as it was called in her childhood days) as she wanted to become a doctor.

Her mother introduced her as a child artiste called Baby Rani at the tender age of six in her own production company called Sangeet Movietone. *'Talaash-e-Haq'* in 1935 thus became Nargis's first movie and that too when she was still studying. Jaddan Bai acted as the heroine opposite Yakub. With this film Jaddan Bai became the first female music director of Bollywood and as a producer-director she produced some more films. Nargis worked as a child artiste in *'Hriday Manthan'* and *'Madam Fashion'* in 1936 and in *'Moti ka Haaar'* a year later.

Nargis played the role of a seventy-five years old woman when she was merely twenty-five years of age. People at large appreciated her role in director Mehboob Khan's *'Mother India'* in 1957 opposite Raj Kumar. She reached the peak of her career with this film. This film became a landmark in the history of Indian cinema. She was the first Indian actress to win an international award for Best Actress at Karlovy Vary in 1956. She was a versatile actress and the first among the film personalities to be conferred with the Padma Shri in 1958. She got married to Sunil Dutt during the shooting of her film *'Mother India'* in which he played the role of her errant son. She gave birth to three children — son Sanjay Dutt and two daughters, Namrata and Priyanka. She has two sons-in-law — Kumar Gaurav and Owen Roncen.

Because of her social activities and services to human kind, she was nominated to the Rajya Sabha in 1980 as Member of Parliament. She won the Filmfare Best Actress Award for *'Mother India'* in 1957. She was adjudged the Best Actress and given the National Film Award for her mature role in her brother's film *'Raat aur Din'* in 1967. She performed a double role in it. She helped her husband in setting up the Ajanta Arts and went to the border areas to entertain the troops posted there. She produced films like *'Mujhe Jeene Do'*, *'Reshma aur Shera'* and *'Yaadein'*. She also assisted her husband in producing the film *'Rocky'* in 1981 to promote her debutant son Sanjay as the hero, but she died before the release of this film which was directed by her husband Sunil Dutt.

Nargis acted as a leading heroine at the age of fourteen in Mehboob Khan's 'Taqdeer' in 1943 opposite veteran actor Motilal. It was released on 31 December 1943 at Roxy Hall, Bombay and became a hit film. Her name was changed from Fatima Rashid to Nargis in this film. A film after her name 'Nargis' was released in 1946 and was produced by Famous Pictures with Rehman as the hero. She acted for the first time opposite Raj Kapoor in 'Aag' in 1948 and subsequently they worked together in fifteen more films, some of which were 'Barsaat' and 'Andaaz' in 1949, 'Awara' in 1951, 'Shri 420' in 1955 and 'Chori Chori', etc. Her last film with Raj Kapoor was 'Jaagte Raho' in 1956. Her pairing with him was most successful and they came to be known as the most romantic pair which was acceptable not only in India but also in the USSR. Her efforts to promote RK Films were unparalleled. She acted in six films with Dilip Kumar — 'Jogan', 'Andaaz', 'Mela', 'Anokha Pyaar', 'Hulchul', and 'Deedar'. The music and lyrics in all her films became very popular during her time. She played in a good number of successful and memorable films The songs in 'Awara', 'Shri 420', 'Mela', 'Deedar' and 'Andaaz' and, above all, of 'Barsaat' still continue to haunt the cine-goers of yesteryears and some of the present generation too. With the success of her films one after another, she became the most sought after actress of Indian cinema.

Nargis, more or less, left working in films after her marriage to Sunil Dutt as she became involved with charitable, social and political causes for upliftment of the spastics for the rest of her life. Unfortunately she died of cancer in 1981. Her husband Sunil Dutt breathed his last on 25 May 2005 at Mumbai while asleep.

* * *

Nutan

Nutan secured the first position in an All India Beauty contest organised in those days when no opportunity was given to the winner to act in films. She was competent enough to perform any kind of role and that too successfully. She was equally adept in portraying light comic roles as she was in serious roles. Her innate simplicity never failed to leave an impact on the minds of her acquaintances. She never used much make-up. Her best films have been 'Seema', 'Bandini', 'Saraswatichandra' and 'Sujata'. She won the Filmfare Awards five times. Simple and unassuming, she was a versatile and accomplished star.

Nutan was born on 4 June 1936 and studied up to Senior Cambridge. She grew up as a complex child. At the peak of her career, she got married in 1959 to Lieutenant Commander Rajneesh Behl and had a son from him. He is Mohnish Behl who is working in films and in TV serials.

Her director-father Kumarsen Samarth introduced her as a teenage girl at the age of nine as a child artiste in his film 'Nal Damayanti' in 1945. Her mother Shobhana Samarth played the lead role opposite Prithivraj Kapoor. When she came of age, her director-producer-mother launched her as a heroine in her own production 'Hamari Beti' in 1950 opposite Shekhar. Shobhana Samarth and her younger daughter Baby Tanuja also worked in the film with Motilal. She then worked in Pancholi Productions' suspense thriller 'Nagina' in 1951 with Nasir Khan, but she was not allowed to enter the theatre as she was underage and was merely fifteen-years old. The film was meant for adults only and it was her first hit film. After working in Amiya Chakravarty's film 'Seema' in 1955 opposite veteran Balraj Sahni, she became a successful star. Her role in the film was most powerful as a rebellious orphan. She won her first Filmfare Award for this film. After her marriage in 1959, she returned to the screen to work in 'Bandini' in 1963 as Kalyani, opposite Ashok Kumar. She was awarded the fourth Filmfare Award for Best Actress for her role in 'Milan' in 1967. She played the role of a tuberculosis patient in 'Hum Log' and as an actress who is cheated by her own people in 'Sone ki Chhidiya'. She did both comic and romantic roles with Dev Anand in 'Paying Guest' and 'Tere Ghar ke Saamane' but her roles in 'Baarish' in 1957 and 'Manzil' in 1960 were very bold and glamorous. She shocked her admirers when for the first time she wore a swimming suit in 'Dilli ka Thug' in 1958, opposite Kishore Kumar. Her roles with Raj Kapoor in 'Chhalia' and in 'Anari' were well applauded. She acted well in super hits like 'Khandaan', 'Milan', 'Meherbaan', 'Gauri' and 'Bhai Behan' made in the south. After working in the super hit film 'Saraswatichandra' in 1968, she became the leadingmost star of Hindi cinema. She performed a brilliant role in 'Saudagar' in 1973 with Amitabh Bachchan.

After 1973, she shifted to acting character roles as a mother in 'Meri Jung' and 'Karma' in 1986 opposite Dilip Kumar. She also played as 'Kaliganj ki Bahu' in the TV serial 'Muzrim Hazir'.

Nutan's memorable films have been 'Hum Log', 'Paying Guest', 'Chhabili', 'Anari', 'Dil Hi to Hai', 'Milan', 'Saudagar', 'Main Tulsi Tere Aangan Ki' in 1978 and 'Jiyo aur Jine Do' in 1982. In the last days of her life she was engaged in a court case against her mother for misappropriation of her life's earnings. After working tirelessly for a long period, she turned weak and was diagnosed as suffering from cancer. She enjoyed a successful and satisfying film career. She died in 1991, leaving behind a long heritage of memorable films behind her.

* * *

Pran

Pran can be termed as life itself for without *pran*, there is no life and the body is dead. Likewise veteran actor Pran had always given his life to films and to heroes in his films. He has performed the character of a villain by getting so immersed in portraying the role that during his hey-days, the mere mention of his name was used to create terror among children. People did not like to name their sons after him. His eyes are still very captivating and continue to breathe fire when he acts as a villain.

Manoj Kumar's film '*Upkar*' in 1967 became a turning point in his film career. He performed a positive role of Malang Chacha and it was well appreciated. He gave a superb performance and his villain's image changed with this film. This was an achievement in his film career and he proved that a villain need not remain a villain forever.

Director Prakash Mehra's '*Zanjeer*' in 1973 with Amitabh Bachchan took him to the zenith of Bollywood. The song '*Yaari hai imaan mera…*', on which he danced as a Pathan, Sher Khan, was executed by him in a most befitting and artistic manner. The song became popular when the film was released. With the super box-office success of this film, he became the most saleable star of the industry. He played a maximum number of films with Amitabh Bachchan as in '*Ganga ki Saugandh*', '*Majboor*', '*Amar Akbar Anthony*', '*Don*', '*Kalia*', '*Naseeb*', '*Inquilab*', '*Sharabi*', '*Mrityudaata*' and '*Tere Mere Sapne*' in 1999.

Pran Krishan Sikand was born on 12 February 1920 at Balimaran in Delhi. His father Lala Keval Krishan Sikand was a civil engineer and his mother Rameshwari gave birth to four sons and three daughters. His father was frequently transferred from one place to another due to which Pran completed his matriculation from Raza High School, Rampur. During the pre-Partition days at Lahore, he worked at the shop of a photographer where he was spotted by storywriter Wali Mohammed, who introduced him to the famous producer, Dalsukh Pancholi. He got a job for a salary of fifty rupees per month by Pancholi Art Pictures. His debut film '*Yamla Jat*' in 1940 was in Punjabi opposite teenager Noorjehan. In this first film, he played the role of a villain. He was signed again for the Punjabi film '*Chaudhry*' in 1941 with Noorjehan and it proved a hit film. His first Hindi film was '*Khandaan*' as hero opposite Noorjehan. He worked in a number of films and was soon established as an upcoming hero. His memorable films are '*Khazanchi*', '*Badnami*', '*Rehana*', '*Do Saudagar*', '*Chunaria*' and '*Nek Dil*' in 1948. He got married to Shukla Ahluwalia at the age of twenty-five years on 18 April 1945 and has three children. He loves reciting and hearing poetry.

Pran arrived a day before Independence in Bombay on 14 August 1947 with wife and son Arvind. He remained jobless for about eight months and was in dire need of money to run his family. The then renowned dancer Cuckoo and writer Sadat Hasan Manto introduced him to Bombay Talkies. His first film at Bombay was '*Ziddi*' in 1948 with Dev Anand and others. Subsequently he acted in Prabhat Pictures' '*Apradhi*' in 1949 with Ram Singh and Madhubala in lead roles. His performance was critically acclaimed. The film '*Badi Bahen*' was a hit.

He has worked with different directors and played different roles and characters. Some of his memorable films are 'Sheesh Mahal' in 1950, 'Afsana', 'Bewafa', 'Aah', 'Biraj Bahu', 'Azad', 'Munimji' in 1955, 'Devdas' in 1956, 'Halaku', 'Jaagte Raho', 'Tumsa Nahin Dekha', 'Madhumati', 'Chhalia', 'Jis Desh Mein Ganga Behati Hai' in 1960, 'Mere Mehboob', 'Kashmir ki Kali', 'Khandaan', 'Shaheed' in 1965, 'Milan', 'Ram aur Shyam', 'Ganwaar' in 1970, 'Heer Ranjha', 'Purab aur Paschim', 'Victoria No. 203', 'Bobby' in 1973, 'Jugnu', 'Sanyaasi', 'Dostana' in 1980, 'Shahenshah' in 1988, 'Suryakant' in 2002 and many more. He has acted in about 400 films so far.

He had played the title role as medieval king in Halaku a with unique get up, a greedy zamindar in 'Madhumati', pimp in 'Adalat', imposter in 'Tumsa Nahin Dekha'. He was a hard core dacoit in 'Jis Desh Mein Ganga Baheti Hai', comic role in 'Victoria No.203' for the first time, in 'Jugnu' he imitated Mujibur Rehman's style and as a lame person in 'Heer Ranjha'. His get up in 'Upkaar' was well appreciated.

He has two sons namely Arvind, Sunil and one daughter Pinky Bhalla. He is the most honourable celebrity in the Bollywood and deserves national recognition for his lifetime contributions in the field of cinema since pre- Independence.

During the Marathi Film Festival in July 2004, he was conferred with the Lifetime Achievement Award. He received the Filmfare Awards for 'Upkaar', 'Aansoo Ban Gaye Phool' and 'Beimaan'. He was conferred with the Padma Bhushan by the government in 2001. He has also received many awards since 1960 from different associations, organisations and clubs.

* * *

Preity Zinta

A girl with a smiling round face, with dimples in her cheeks and called Preity Zinta took the celluloid world by a storm on entering this industry. Her mother is her foundation and she is the most important person in her life. Her father expired in a car accident when she was just thirteen-years old. She used to be known as Daddy's girl and his death marked a turning point in her life. She studied at Shimla and topped in English literature. She shot to fame as the refreshing, cool, drenched model in the Liril advertisement and came to be called the 'Liril girl'. She was studying criminal psychology in Bombay University when Shekhar Kapoor, the famous director, saw her Liril ad and the Cadbury's Perk ad where she has a mischievous expression and twinkling eyes. He decided to cast her in his next film. Preity signed the contract with him but the planned film 'Tara Rum Rum' is still pending with the director.

Preity is quite different from the present crowd of film actresses. She came into limelight when she modelled with Aamir Khan in the Coke ad. She was introduced to Bollywood by director Mani Ratnam. Her debut film was 'Dil Se' in 1998 and in it she performed the supporting actress's role of an unconventional fiancée by acting against the established actress Manisha Koirala. She made a mark with her acting in this film, but the latter flopped. For the first time she acted as a leading actress in 'Soldier' in 1998. It was a hit film. Her role in the film was well appreciated for she possesses the talent required. She has proved her ability to act well in all the films she has acted in so far, such as 'Kya Kehna Hai' in 2000, 'Har Dil jo Pyaar Karega', 'Mission Kashmir', 'Dillagi', 'Sangharsh', 'Farz', 'Chori Chori Chupke Chupke', 'Yeh Raaaste Hain Pyaar Ke', 'Dil ne Jise Apna Kaha', 'Lakshya' and 'Veer Zara'. 'Veer Zara' in 2004 was a challenging role as she had never played a role where she is old and dressed all the time in Indian clothes. Her performance was superb and unbelievable. The film became a super hit at the box-office. Her next film 'Chori Chori Chupke Chupke' emphasized the importance of sacrifice in a relationship. Before doing this film, she visited a whole lot of bars and pubs to prepare herself for her role as a prostitute in this film. Farhan Akhtar's 'Lakshya' was a war film where she inspired the hero to become something in life. Her acting was energetic and lively. Her modern outlook and bewitching personality make her a favourite with the masses.

'Dil Chahta Hai' in 2001 mirrors the life of the city youth, but 'Koi Mil Gaya' and 'Kal Ho Na Ho' established her as one of the top actresses in the film world. She has acted in two Telugu films also — 'Premante Idera' in 1998 and in 'Raja Kumarudu' in 1999. Her role as an unwed mother in 'Salaam Namaste' in 2005 has been remarkable and the film was declared a hit. In this film the reality about a relationship in today's world is depicted. The greatest contributors to her career are her self-confidence and hard work. According to her, a competent director is able to extract a good performance from any artiste irrespective of the circumstances. She wants richer experiences, better relationships and to be a part of better films. She wants children, a family, more passion and more life. She is a woman of the world, representing the independent, self-willed face of the present Bollywood.

Preity Zinta has worked with different directors on different subjects with all seriousness and dedication. Within a very short period she has carved a niche for herself. With an array of successful films behind her, she is on the top of the world. She is not interested in doing more than a couple of films at one time. According to her, no actor is bigger that a script and no star is bigger than a film. She was conferred the Filmfare Best Debut Award in 1999 and the Filmfare Award for the Best Actress for Karan Johar's *Kal Ho Na Ho* in 2004. It was her seventeenth film.

Preity Zinta even participated in a Temptation World Tour with Shah Rukh Khan and others. She has rightly established herself in the film world and also in the hearts of the discerning public.

* * *

Prem Chopra

Prem Chopra

Prem Chopra started his career as a circulation supervisor in a publishing house in Bombay in 1950. Born in Lahore and brought up in Shimla, he did graduation in arts from Punjab University. None could have guessed at that time that this young man would become a film star and that too as a prominent villain. He was, however, keen to become an actor, so after office hours he used to visit various theatres. After many attempts, he could succeed in getting chance to play the title role in a Punjabi film 'Chaudhary Karnail Singh', which won the National Award. This helped him to establish himself in the film industry, and subsequently, he acted in many Hindi and Punjabi films.

Prem Chopra successfully played the roles of a villain in 'Teesri Manzil' in 1966 and in Manoj Kumar's 'Upkar', and both the films were proved to be hits, which brought him fame as a villain-star, and subsequently he was flooded with offers to act as a villain in several other films, and that forced him to leave his job, and join films as a full time career. In 1965, he played the role of Sukhdev in the film 'Shaheed' (based on the life of martyr Bhagat Singh), and this was one of his rare positive roles. His films 'Khiladi', 'Aaj ka Gundaraj', 'Deewana', 'Phool Bane Angaarey' and 'Dastaan' in which he appeared as a villain, and the films were successful. And these successes brought him many more films, where he not only played negative roles but also as a good man. Some films depicting his positive roles were 'Khiladi', 'Jagriti', 'Prem Tapasya', and 'Ghar Jamai'.

Prem Chopra has been in the film industry for the last 44 years.and still he is a busy artist. He has always been a dedicated artist and achieved appreciations for his roles. In the film 'Sanam tere hain hum' he enacted a song sung by Michael Jackson, which added further to his popularity, though the film was not successful at box-office. In Raj Kapoor's 'Bobby' in 1973, his dialogue 'Prem, Prem hai mera naam& ' became very popular, and that was the peak time of his film career. In years to come, he performed memorable villainous roles in films like 'Trishul' in 1978, 'Kala Patthar' in 1979, 'Do Anjaane', 'Aas Pass', 'Kala Sona' etc etc.. These films were hits of their times at the box-office, and that made him so eminent that many films could sell on the basis of his name alone.

His dialogue like 'Main woh bala hoon jo sheeshe se patthar ko tor de' won him credits and applause from the masses, even though he was a bad man in many films. With the changing trends in Hindi cinema, he is now enacting character roles in several films, like Aishwarya Rai's father in Radheshyam Sitaram.

Prem Chopra is a prolific reader, an amateur poet and has authored many Urdu couplets. With a very happy family life, he is the father of three married daughters, and is closely related with Kapoor family.

* * *

Prithviraj Kapoor

The torchbearer of the Kapoor family was none other than Prithviraj who was born on 3 November 1906 in Samundari, a village located between Peshawar and Rawalpindi in Pakistan. His father Pathan Bashesharnath Kapoor was in the police service while his grandfather Dewan Keshovmal Kapoor was a *tehsildar* in Samundari. His mother died when he was only three-years old. He was brought up by his grandfather. He graduated from King Edward College in Peshawar where he acted in some plays. His first appearance on the college stage was invariably in the role of a woman. His stepmother loved him as if he was her own son. He was married to Ramsarni at the age of seventeen while he was still studying. He had an intense desire to become an actor but his father was dead against it as he considered actors as '*kanjar*'.

Prithviraj mustered up courage at the age of twenty-one to go to Bombay in 1928, leaving behind his wife Ramsarni and children in Peshawar to fulfil his dream. Raj Kapoor was born in 1924 in Peshawar and was about five-years old at the time. He stayed at Kashmir Hotel with a paltry seventy-five rupees in his pocket. He somehow managed to enter the Imperial Studios of Ardeshir Irani and initially worked as an extra on a daily wages of two and a half rupees in silent films— '*Challenge*' in 1929, '*Wedding Night*' and '*Dao Pech*' for a few days. One day, when he stood in a queue of extras, actress Ermelin spotted this fair, tall man with Roman nose and selected him for the male lead role opposite her in the film '*Cinema Girl*' in 1930. The film flopped but it provided him the impetus to work hard to succeed.

Thereafter he never looked back and became the thespian of the Indian film industry. He was the most handsome, tall and well-built hero of the time and blessed with a powerful voice. He joined films when the cinema was still finding its feet. His first full-length talkie was director Ardeshir Irani's '*Alam Ara*' in 1931 in which he played the role of actress Zubeida's father. Prior to this, he had worked in films '*Prince Vijay Kumar*', '*Sher-e-Arab*' in 1930, '*Namak Haram Kaun*', '*Bar ke Pohar*', '*Golibar*', '*A Bid for the Throne*' and '*Toofan*' in 1931 — all silent films. When he started receiving a monthly salary of seventy rupees a month, his wife and children joined him at Tardeo, Bombay in 1929.

He was one of the most talented actors of his time and saw the journey of the Indian cinema from the silent era to the talkie era. He was the first celebrity from the industry to be nominated for Rajya Sabha as Member of Parliament for five years from 1952 to 1957. He was a man with simple tastes. He had a weakness for theatre since an early age. After doing a number of films he did not feel satisfied, so he joined the Grant Anderson Theatrical Company which toured from place to place enacting live plays on the stage. He was already a popular film star before joining the theatre. He acted in the play '*Hamlet*' during his tour to Calcutta in 1932.

At Calcutta he joined New Theatres and played some memorable roles in films like '*Raj Rani Meera*' in 1933, '*Daku Mansoor*' in 1934, '*Manzil*' in 1936, '*President*', '*Vidyapati*' in 1937, '*Abhagin*' in 1938 and '*Dushman*' in 1939. He also played the role of Rama in '*Seeta*', '*Ramayana*' in 1934 and '*Milap*' in 1937. He again left for Bombay in 1939 to work with Ranjit

Movietone's films 'Adhuri Kahani' in 1939, 'Aaj ka Hindustan' and 'Pagal' in 1940. He was the first actor to start freelancing instead of working on a monthly salary. He became free to work on his own terms and conditions. He did a number of films including actor-producer-director Sohrab Modi's film 'Sikander' in 1941 and powerfully played the role of the Greek king. It proved a hit and the most memorable film of his career.

After doing a good number of films, he once again returned to the stage, his first love. Ultimately on 15 January 1944, he founded the Prithvi Theatres. The first play 'Shakuntala' was staged on 9 March 1945 and his son Raj, who was just nineteen-years old, managed the affairs of backstage, Shammi Kapoor played as Bharat and Shashi Kapoor acted in a crowd scene. He established a new trend in Hindustani Theatre at a time when Parsi Theatre was ruling the era. Subsequently he staged a number of plays like 'Pathan', 'Ghaddar', etc. After staging plays for sixteen long years, he had no alternative but to close down his beloved Prithvi Theatres in May 1960 due to financial reasons.

Prithviraj acted in some memorable films like 'Pardesi' in 1957, 'Rustam Sohrab' in 1963, 'Rajkumar' in 1964, 'Sikandar-e-Azam' in 1965, 'Insaaf ka Mandir' in 1969 and 'Heer Ranjha' in 1970.

He died of cancer on 29 May 1972 and his wife Ramsarni Kapoor followed him just after sixteen days of his death on 14 June 1972. He ruled the film world for about forty years. He was honoured in 1969 with the Padma Bhushan and was posthumously conferred the Dada Saheb Phalke Award in 1971. He often used to say, "Nature determines the right moment for everything."

* * *

Raj Kapoor

Born in Peshawar as Ranbir Raj Kpaoor to father Prithviraj Kapoor and mother Ramasarni Devi on 14 December 1924, he had his early education in Calcutta. After passing matriculation, he decided not to study further. The family environment was such that the stage and films constituted his life due to his father.

Ranbir Raj Kapoor started his career on the stage with his illustrious father. A strikingly handsome and ambitious Prithviraj Kapoor arrived in Bombay in 1929, appeared in the film '*Alam Ara*', the first Indian talkie, and toured the country staging Shakespeare's plays. In 1944, he formed the Prithvi Theatres, which still functions today under the supervision of his other actor-son, Shashi Kapoor. Another son is Shammi Kapoor who too is an actor.

Ranbir Raj Kapoor was married to Krishna, sister of actor Prem Nath. He has three sons, namely Randhir, Rishi and Rajiv Kapoor. His daughter Ritu got married in the Nanda family of Delhi and whose son married Shweta, daughter of Amitabh Bachchan. His grand daughters Karishma and Kareena are established heroines in Bollywood.

Ranbir Raj now famous as Raj Kapoor acted as a child artiste in director Devki Bose's film '*Inquilab*' in 1935 at the age of eleven. He worked as a clapper boy at the age of seventeen. He did an important role in a film made by Bombay Talkies — '*Hamari Baat*' in 1943 with Devika Rani, Jairaj and Suraiya. At the same time, he exhibited his acting calibre by doing an important role in director Kidar Sharma's film, '*Gauri*' in 1943 with Prithviraj Kapoor and Monika Desai. He became assistant to director Kidar Sharma who later on gave him the first break as a hero in his film '*Neel Kamal*' in 1947 with debutant Madhubala, the Venus of Indian Cinema. Director-producer Bhalji Pendhaerkar made Raj Kapoor his assistant in his film '*Valimki*' in 1944. During these years, he learnt all about filmmaking. He performed on stage as a clown in the drama '*Shakuntala*' and as Ramu, the servant, in a controversial drama '*Deewar*' produced by his father. He even sang songs with Suraiya and musician Madan Mohan. He acted in and sang the song '*O duniya ke rahne walon…*' in '*Dil ki Rani*' and '*Piya milan ko naveli jaye re…*' in '*Jail Yatra*' in 1947.

He acted, produced and directed his first film '*Aag*' in 1948 at the age of twenty-three only. Singer Mukesh sang one of the best songs of his life — '*Zinda hook is tarah ke game zindage nahin…*' in this film. Nargis was an established star by now and acted for the first time opposite him. Raj Kapoor himself made a moving comment on their first film of his, "I'll never forget '*Aag*' because it was the story of a youth consumed by the desire for a brighter and more intense life."

Raj Kapoor became a star with the release of Mehboob Khan's '*Andaaz*' made in 1949. This was the first and last film of Nargis and Dilip Kumar together with him. His second directorial venture was the musical super-hit film '*Barsaat*' made in 1949. In this film he showed moral decadence in conflict with integrity; truth with falsehood; Pran, the romantic-idealist with Gopal, the ruthless rationalist. And weaving it together were two separate tales of love and loyalty, one ending in death, the other in happiness. The music, a lively integration of Western and Indian, enhanced the mood of quiet melancholy created so ably by the black-and-white photography of Jal Mistry. It was in this film that he introduced Ramanand Sagar, Shailendra, Hasrat Jaipuri, Prem Nath and Nimmi. Music directors Shanker and Jaikishan acquired a firm foothold with this film and their melodious songs became most popular in those days and still haunt the masses, like, for example, the song 'Hawa mein udta jaye mora lal dupatta malmal ka…' He established his own RK Studio in 1950 with the earnings from his film 'Barsaat'. Covering an area of four acres, RK Studio began in 1950 at Chembur, then a remote and sparsely inhabited suburb of Bombay. The first stint of shooting was done even before the walls and ceilings were in place. An incredible dream sequence of 'Awara', Raj Kapoor's third film to be released in 1951, was shot here. The sequence marked the beginning of his involvement and experiments with the spectacular and grandiose. Raj Kapoor, with the super success of this film and 'Shree 420' in 1955, touched the zenith of Indian cinema. The film 'Awara' and its mesmerising song 'Awara hun…' was a super hit in India and Russia. The film dealt with the question of what forms an individual's moral grounding, i.e. nurture or nature and was interspersed with comedy and stirring love scenes. It stormed its way into the hearts of the audience from the East. Raj Kapoor and Nargis became household names in the bazaars of the Arab world, while the Soviets made a widespread distribution of the film dubbed in a number of languages. In 'Shree 420' made in 1955, he addressed the raging issues of poverty, unemployment and national pride in the new Indian state while maintaining the audience interest in the romantic plot. While never revolutionary in tone, many of his films explored the ability of the individual to overcome economic and environmental injustice while maintaining his/her innocence and integrity. He is quoted as believing that the individual's struggles ultimately lead to the desire for love, to care and be cared for and this was in keeping with his admiration of Charlie Chaplin. Kapoor's own 'tramp' image in 'Awara', 'Shree 420', 'Mera Naam Joker' in 1970 were modelled on his idol, though with a definite individual flair.

The last named film took six years in the making; it was also three hours long, cost a fortune, and Raj Kapoor staked everything he possessed on the project. The script, once again by K.A. Abbas, was an impressionistic interpretation of Raj Kapoor's own life. It was meant to be like Chaplin's 'Limelight', but being Raj Kapoor and, by now definitely larger than life, it was three films in one — a complete and complicated biography in three parts, spectacular to the point of being distracting. Yet it was far more interesting in parts than the formula-ridden 'Sangam', which he had made in 1964. In the last named film Raj Kapoor made extensive use of locations in Europe, providing his audience with the thrill of a tour abroad. For five years the film held the record for being the biggest box-office grosser in the history of Indian cinema. Immensely successful throughout the Middle East, it was supposed to have run simultaneously for several years in both Israel and Egypt.

Raj Kapoor was a romantic person and never ditched love either in life or in films. His pairing with Nargis in sixteen films was one of the most successful in the history of Hindi cinema and their last film was 'Chori Chori' in 1956. He also made another film with a guest appearance by Nargis in 'Jagte Raho' and it received the Grand Prix at the Karlovy Vary Film Festival in 1958.

Three years later, when Raj Kapoor directed 'Bobby' with his son Rishi and a new face, Dimple

Kapadia, no one expected much from the film. But it became a runaway hit, for its appeal was to the new generation of a changing India just as his earlier films had appealed to the post-war Indian youth.

His films demonstrated an ear for music and direction that continues to influence Bollywood filmmaking to this day. His understanding of the musical feel of his movies gave his storytelling style a fluidity equal to that of the best American movie musicals. He surrounded himself with the foremost talents in filmmaking, acting, writing, like Khwaja Ahmad Abbas, music composers like Shanker and Jaikishan and playback singers like Mukesh, Mohammad Rafi and Lata Mangeshkar. Raj Kapoor continued to make films of very critical and popular success till his death in 1988 and apparently considered 'Mera Naam Joker' his personal favourite. The film was shot artistically but proved a great disaster and he became nearly bankrupt. He then made 'Satyam Shivam Sundaram' in 1978 and it was one of his best films. Unlike 'Bobby' it exploited an earlier theme, that of 'Aag'. Roopa, disfigured by fire, had to suffer heartbreak and tragedy before her inner beauty is revealed to the man she loves. The next directorial venture was the film 'Prem Rog' set in post-Independence India when the feudal traditions were still oppressively alive. A carefree young girl married into a class-conscious Thakur family, loses her husband in an accident immediately after the wedding. Spoilt and protected in her childhood, she suddenly faces the deprivations of a Hindu widow's life. In 1985 he made another glamour-filled film with son Rajeev Kapoor and Mandakini 'Ram Teri Ganga Maili'.

He was a well-known name not only in India, but also in the Middle East, South-east Asia and eastern Europe. His sons are trying to maintain the RK Films banner by producing a film or two once in a while. He was the greatest showman of his time in Bollywood. He had presented his heroines in a most bewitching, glamorous, voluptuous and exotic roles in his films.

He was conferred the Dada Saheb Phalke Award on 2 May 1988 by the President of India in New Delhi. During the investiture ceremony, he fell sick and was rushed to the hospital but he could not survive the heart attack and died on 2 June 1988. Out of his seventy-one films, he produced eighteen films under the RK banner and directed-edited only seven films. He was conferred the Padma Bhushan by the President of India on 5 October 1971. It is very difficult to find as talented a person in the Hindi film industry to match the multifaceted personality of the great showman like Raj Kapoor. He acted as a clapper boy, stage artist, actor, producer, director and the only studio-owner at the age of twenty-six years. He had an unbelievable sense of music and melody. He introduced a number of new faces for the first time in his films. A good number of his films were box-office successes. He was a mastermind in presenting serious social issues in a light manner and with enduring appeal. His zest and passion for cinema made him one of the greatest showmen of this medium.

* * *

Rani Mukherjee

Rani Mukherjee made her debut with the film 'Raja ki Aayegi Baraat' which was a low-budget film. Despite turning out to be a damp squib at the box-office, it did get her some rave reviews. She acted opposite the hero Shadaab Khan, who is son of the late Amjad Khan. She played the role of a miserable wife and the film flopped, leaving no impact on the public. She won recognition only after working in her first successful film 'Ghulam' in 1998 as the Khandala girl. In this film she acted opposite Aamir Khan and by singing the song 'Aati kya Khandala...' this light-eyed beauty became not only known as the Khandala girl but found a large following among the youngsters.

Born on 21 March 1978 at Mumbai, she draws her lineage from an illustrious film family. Ram Mukherjee, her father, who directed films like 'Leader' and 'Hum Hindustani' in the sixties and her mother used to be a playback singer. Her grandfather S. Mukherjee was a renowned film director-producer. She is a normal girl and looks like a next-door girl. She is five feet three inches tall and conversant with Bengali, English and Hindi. Her aunt Debashree Roy is a well-known Bengali actress and of course, her most famous star connection is with Kajol and her younger sister Tanisha who are her cousins. She believes in God, loves to eat fish and non-vegetarian food and possesses a husky voice that her audiences love. She models for some popular consumer products too. She has taken no training in either stage or theatre acting and no formal education from a film institute.

In the early days of her career, Rani had to struggle in films, particularly with the 'Kajol's cousin' tag sticking to her for a long time. Her striking screen presence caught the fancy of a very important director, Karan Johar who offered her a role that many a star had turned down. The film 'Kuch Kuch Hota Hai' was made in 1998 and she acted opposite Shah Rukh Khan. She was pitted against her cousin Kajol, who was already famous for her spontaneous and inhibition-free acting. While Kajol was beyond doubt the film's heroine, Rani Mukherjee too had her share of success in the supporting role as Shah Rukh Khan's first wife. The film was a box-office hit and made her commercially viable. The film was conferred with the Filmfare Award too.

The public began to notice her, wondering what exactly made Rani Mukherjee click — her dancing, dare bare clothes, her husky voice, her light-brown eyes or the little peek you got of her acting abilities. In any case she was putting in all her effort to succeed as an actress. Riding high on the success of 'Ghulam' and 'Kuch Kuch Hota Hai', she began to draw producers and directors who made a beeline for her door. A film like 'Baadal' did cast a shadow on her prospects as the film left the theatre in India without a whimper. The same fate awaited 'Had Kar di Aapne' in which she acted with Govinda, a very popular hero of the period. It was a comedy made by David Dhawan but it failed to raise a laugh or make the cash boxes ring.

Rani Mukherjee tried to remain unfazed. She then acted in Kamal Hasan's film 'Hey Ram', but it did not propel her career to the extent she expected. There was no critical appreciation of her performance; in reality her fans were disappointed to see her locked in a kiss with Kamal Hasan in the film, though Rani Mukherjee had no qualms about it: "I wanted to work with Mr Kamal Hasan. The rest did not matter," she is said to have spoken in an interview. Nevertheless even a dud like the

film 'Hello Brother' could not affect her newfound status. Directors like Inder Kumar were soon begging for dates and half a dozen other producers were waiting in the wings to sign her up.

With every new release of the film, she learnt new techniques, style of powerful dialogue delivery and film mannerisms. Her films 'Mehndi' in 1998 and 'Brother' and 'Mann' in 1999 the last named in which she appeared as a sexy girl in the song 'Kali nagin ke…' and in 'Hey Ram' in 2000 were not really successful films. Other films during the year 2000, 'Khahin Pyaar no ho Jaaye', 'Har Dil Jo Pyaar Karega' and 'Bichhoo' also did not do well commercially. She acted in films like 'Chori Chori Chupke Chupke', 'Bas Itna sa Khwaab Hai', 'Nayak', 'The Real Hero', 'Kabhi Khushi Kabhi Gham' in 2001, 'Chalo Ishq Ladaayein', 'Saathiya', 'Mujhse Dosti Karoge', 'Pyaar Diwana Hota Hai' in 2002 and finally decided not to do many films at a time.

Her successful films in the year 2003 were 'LoC-Kargil', 'Kal Ho Na Ho' (with a special appearance), 'Chori Chori' and 'Chalte Chalte'. For 'Hum Tum' in 2004, she was given the Filmfare Award for Best Actress and in the same year she was declared the Best Actress in a supporting role for the film 'Yuva' in 2004. The film was however mediocre.

Rani Mukherjee's subsequent films like 'Veer Zara' in 2004 and 'Black' in 2005 have the best and successful films at the box-office. In 'Black' she brilliantly performed the role of a handicapped girl with Amitab Bachchan, who was deaf, dumb and blind. Her role will be remembered and cherished for ages to come. In 'Veer Zara' her role as a Pakistani advocate who defends prisoner Shah Rukh Khan has proved her to be a superb actress of Bollywood. The film even helped in creating harmony between India and Pakistan. The film won many awards in the country. The other film 'Bunty aur Babli' in 2005 was a light entertaining film with Amitabh and Abhishek Bachchan acting in it. It proved successful particularly due to the melodious song 'Kajrare kajrare…' Her film 'Paheli', shot in Rajasthan with Shah Rukh Khan acting opposite her was nominated for the Oscar award. The role in the film 'The Rising: Ballad of Mangal Pandey' with Aamir Khan is another feather in her crown.

She has participated in live stage programmes with Shah Rukh Khan at Las Vegas and other places. She is a complete family girl. She donated an amount of five lakh rupees to tsunami relief work in Tamil Nadu for the Prime Minister's Relief Fund. Her pending projects are 'Sanwariya', 'Babul' and others.

* * *

Rekha

Rekha

Rekha means a straight line but Rekha, the actress, has always led a life which has been ziz-zag. Her dusky charm and sharp penetrating eyes are her outstanding features. She became a sizzling-hot actress as soon as she switched to Hindi cinema from the Tamil film world. She is the daughter of superstar of Tamil films, Gemini Ganesan and actress Pushpavalli, both of whom were successful film stars in Tamil cinema.

Rekha was born in 1954 and started acting in films at the age of thirteen. She made her debut in her aunt Anjali Devi's film 'Ammakosam'. She moved to Bombay when she left her studies due to financial constraints. She was not conversant with Hindi language or with dancing. Blessed with a sharp mind, she learnt Hindi and dance within a few months. Her debut Hindi film was producer-director Mohan Sehgal's 'Sawan Bhadon' in 1970 opposite Navin Nishcol. This film was an instant hit and she marked her presence in Bollywood with a bang. In course of time she developed her Hindi dialogue delivery and through sincere and sustained efforts coupled with hard work became one of the most versatile actresses of Bollywood. She became the talk of the town when she kissed Biswajeet during the shooting of a film in which both starred. Though the scene was censored in the film, the photograph was published on the cover of Life magazine. She acted in 'Dost aur Dushman' in 1971 and in 'Rampur ka Lakshman' in 1972.

Her career took off when she acted opposite the legendary star Amitabh Bachchan in 'Namak Haram' in 1973. Her pairing with him continued for a pretty long time till Yash Chopra's 'Silsila' in 1981. Their pairing became the most successful and talked about affair in Bollywood. Their most memorable films have been 'Do Ajanabi' in 1976, 'Alaap' in 1977, 'Imaan Dharam' in 1977, 'Khoon Pasina', 'Muqaddar ka Sikander' in 1978, 'Mr Natwar Lal' in 1979 and 'Suhaag'. She worked in Hrishikesh Mukherjee's film 'Khubsoorat' in 1980 in a very hilarious role and won the Filmfare Award for Best Actress. Her most memorable role however has been in Muzaffar Ali's 'Umrao Jaan' in 1981 in which she played a courtesan and held the audiences spellbound with her performance. She won the National Award for this film. She also played supporting roles in 'Mujhe Insaaf Chahiye' in 1983, 'Zameen Aasmaan' in 1984, 'Kalyug' in 1980, 'Vijeta' in 1983 and 'Utsav' in 1984. The film 'Utsav' was a classical and costume film.

Rekha then went into hibernation and made her comeback entry forcefully with 'Khoon Bhari Maang' in 1988, which was a remake of 'Return to Eden'. She was conferred the Filmfare Award for Best Actress for this film. Her other film, 'Phool Bane Angarey' in 1991, was a hit and critics acclaimed it. She played the role of a vamp in Umesh Mehra's 'Khiladiyon ke Khiladi' in 1996 with Akshay Kumar in the lead. She proved her talent at this stage once again. She won the Filmfare Award for Best Supporting Actress in this film. Her brilliant role as a priestess of sex in Mira Nair's film 'Kamasutra' in 1998 was well appreciated. Her other memorable roles were in 'Qila', 'Mother', 'Lajja' and 'Zubeida'. She proved in 2005 that she is still a force to be reckoned with in the film world against the young stars in her latest release, 'Bach ke Rehna re Baba'. She has not married and leads a lonely life.

* * *

Saif Ali Khan

Chhote Nawab or Saif Ali Khan is the new successful star of Bollywood. He was born on 16 August 1970 in Delhi to former Indian cricketer Nawab Mansur Ali Khan Pataudi and mother Sharmila Tagore, who is a veteran actress of Bollywood. His young sister Soha Ali Khan has registered her entry into Bangla and Hindi films.

Saif married actress Amrita Singh, who was twelve years senior to him and has two children, daughter Sarah and son Ibrahim. He has divorced his wife and is currently seen with his latest flame Roza, an Italian by birth. During his childhood, his mother used to be particular about his discipline and father about his education, etc. He studied at Cathedral School, Mumbai and then migrated to Winchester, UK where he learnt to play the guitar, write poetry and expand his creative activities.

Saif's debut film was director Yash Chopra's 'Parampara' in 1993 which was an action-packed love story based on rivalry between two families. After this film, he acted in a number of ordinary films for eight to nine years, but sheer determination and perseverance helped him to stick on in the industry. He had wanted to be taken seriously as an actor and he tried to act to the best of his ability in films like 'Yeh Dillagi', and 'Main Khiladi Tu Anari' with Akshay Kumar and their film ultimately became a successful hit at the box-office. His other films like 'Sambandh', 'Keemat' and 'Bombai ka Babu' flopped.

Saif however performed a memorable role in producer Vidhu Vinod Chopra's film 'Parineeta' in 2005 opposite newcomer Vidya Balan and veteran Sanjay Dutt. The film was critically acclaimed. Prior to this film, he had to his credit successful films like Yash Chopra's 'Hum Tum' in 2004, Karan Johar's 'Kal Ho Na Ho' in 2003 and Farhan Akhtar's 'Dil Chahta Hai' in 2001. He won the National Film Award for 'Hum Tum'. His style, appearance and dialogue delivery in 'Dil Chahta Hai' were unique and different and happily accepted by the masses. In Ram Gopal Verma's 'Ek Haseena Thi' he was serious but striking. He became a successful star of the modern era. Subsequently his 'Salaam Namaste' in 2005 opposite Preity Zinta proved a super hit film. His first song-free English film 'Being Cyrus' was a touching comedy presenting the tale of six colourful characters. It was a different kind of non-mainstream cinema.

Saif even tried his hand at playback singing in 'Hum Saath Saath Hain' in 1999. So far he has done about fifty films and taken many world tours for participating in shows abroad in the last twelve years. He has many projects of renowned producers and directors in hand and these are awaiting release. His other memorable films are 'Dil Tera Diwana', 'Biwi No.1', 'Darna Mana Hai' and 'LoC-Kargil' in 2003.

* * *

Salman Khan

Salman Khan

Salman Khan is one of the most successful stars of Bollywood today. He is one of Indian cinema s hottest selling stars   a safe bet any day.

Born on 27 December 1965 in Mumbai to father Salim Khan, a famous script-writer and to mother Salam who is a Hindu, he has two brothers, Arbaaz and Sohail, both turned-director. Salman also has a step-mother, Helen, the one and only cabaret dancer of the Indian screen to dance without inhibition and beautifully at that.

He studied in Bandra and was a good sportsman and swimmer in school. He was poor in his studies and was very keen on joining the film industry. He worked for some time with Hotel Sea Rock in Bandra before joining as an assistant director with Shashi Lal Nair during the making of *Falak* .

He subsequently made an unconventional debut as Farooque Sheikh s younger brother in *Biwi Ho to Aisi* in 1988 but went unnoticed in the film world at that stage. The film had the evergreen Rekha as the leading heroine in the film. The following year came *Maine Pyaar Kiya* and this changed his life forever. Sooraj Barjatya s syrupy romance turned Salman Khan into a teen icon. The film was a simple love story produced by Rajshri and in which he acted with a new heroine, Bhagyashree; both became celebrities after the release of this film all over India. The film earned box-office success instantly. Salman became a hot-selling star of the era. Every producer with money in his pocket wanted to sign the star on the dotted line.

Be it Sooraj Barjatya, or Sanjay Bhansali or even David Dhawan, they waited to sign him for their films. In 1994, though Madhuri Dixit, the most successful actress of the Hindi screen of her time, walked off with the accolades for her mesmeric presence in *Hum Aapke Hain Kaun* , it was to Salman s credit that he gracefully played the second fiddle and let her hog the show. All this was followed by some action films like Rakesh Roshan s *Karan Arjun* and K.K. Singh s *Veergati* and *Pyaar Kiya to Darna Kya* to succeed at the box-office. He then acted in Sanjay Bhansali's *Khamoshi* in 1996 which revealed his acting abilities for the first time as a sensitive music composer who loves Manisha Koirala, the daughter of deaf and dumb parents.

Finally came *Hum Dil de Chuke Sanam* in 1999 which proved a tremendously successful film. Within ten years of his making his debut film, he began to be ranked as the topmost star of Bollywood. He got a special guest role in *Kuch Kuch Hota Hai* in 1998. He has also acted in *Maine Pyar Kyon Kiya* , *No Entry* , 'Kyonki', 'Shaadi Kar Phas Gaya Yaar' and *Saawan* . He worked in Abbas Mastan s film *Chori Chori Chupke Chupke* in 2001 with Rani Mukherjee and Preity Zinta. This multi starrer proved a hit film. He even acted under the direction of Dev Anand in *Love at Times Square* , but it was an average film. His film *No Entry* proved a super hit. His films with David Dhawan like *Deewana Mastana* , in which he gave a guest appearance and *Dulhan Hum Le Jayenge* , *Chal Mere Bhai* and *yeh Hai Jalwa* cemented his image and his popularity grew with every film that he acted in. He has even been called the star of David Dhawan . Apart from many other films, he acted in *Mujhse Shaadi Karoge* in 2004 and in *Phir Milenge* based on AIDS patients, but both these films bombed at the box-office. He acted in his brother-in-law s film

'*Dil ne Jise Apna Kaha*' with Preity Zinta, based on a love story developed under the shadow of terrorism and shot in the intense cold temperature of Russia.

Salman Khan acted in director Ravi Chopra's film '*Baghban*' in which he gave a unique and commendable performance as an adopted son.

According to Salman he is not afraid of speaking the truth and his strength lies in his honesty. He loves children and often visits children afflicted by AIDS and cancer. He even auctioned a 24-carat gold trophy to donate the amount to a home for the aged.

What is most surprising about him is that he never fails to remain away from the limelight, or for driving rashly and knocking down people or for killing endangered animals. In what must have been the ugliest time of his public life, Salman Khan was arrested in Rajasthan in 1998 while shooting for Sooraj Barjatya's film '*Hum Saath Saath Hain*'. He was charged of hunting down the black buck deer. After spending a few days in a local prison, he was released much to the film industry's relief. The court case was filed by the Bishnoi community of Rajasthan for poaching black buck in Jodhpur. On 10 April 2006, he was given rigorous imprisonment for five years but was granted bail on April 30. His activities apart, he will continue to remain in the news for time to come.

* * *

Sanjay Dutt

The renowned and respected actress Nargis of yesteryears gave birth to her first child Sanjay or 'Sanju Baba' on 29 July 1959. He was born with a silver spoon in his mouth and entered the film world with a golden axe in his hand. He has two younger sisters Namrata, who is married to former jubilee star Rajendra Kumar's son, and Priya, who a Member of Parliament. His father Sunil Dutt was a radio journalist, actor, social activist, successful politician, Member of Parliament from Mumbai and Sports Minister in the Central Government. Father Sunil Dutt died of a heart attack on 25 May 2005. Sanjay's mother Nargis died of cancer before the release of Sanjay's debut film 'Rocky' in 1981 and directed by his father Sunil Dutt. Nargis was very keen to see this film but Fate had ordained otherwise. The film was a hit but it failed to establish him as a star.

Sanjay had been very attached to his mother Nargis and went into a long period of depression because of his mother's death. He married Richa Sharma but again his life was filled with anguish and pain when it was discovered that Richa too had cancer. Richa, like her mother-in-law, died of cancer leaving behind a daughter, Trishla. Sanjay is fighting a court battle with his in-laws for the custody of his daughter.

Sanjay has faced many tragedies in his life. He left for USA for treatment at a drug rehabilitation centre in America. He was charged for illegal possession of AK-57 arms during 1993. He was imprisoned and put behind bars under TADA and the case is still continuing. After political intervention, he was granted conditional bail.

Director Mahesh Bhatt and producer Kumar Gaurav gave him a fresh opportunity in their film 'Naam' in 1986, wherein they could make Sanjay portray the inner pain and anguish by giving a powerful performance. With so much of pain, tension, litigation and humiliation in life, anybody else could have broken down but Sanjay faced the struggles of life stoically to survive it all.

He slowly began to build his career with 'Saajan' in 1991 and in which he acted as a lame poet and showed his remarkable personality for the first time. In 'Sadak' in 1991, he acted as a taxi-driver who fights against an underworld don. It was an action-oriented film and Sanjay performed the stunts himself. The film created the image of Sanjay as a powerful action hero. Producer-director Subhash Gahai, in his film 'Khalnayak' in 1993, presented Sanjay as a miscreant and made him act opposite Madhuri Dixit and whom she reforms in the end in the movie. It was a successful film. The release of this film coincided with Sanjay's arrest in connection with the 1993 bomb blasts in Mumbai. Sanjay spent over a year in jail during which time public sympathy for this ill-fated actor reached a crescendo. Sanjay was charged in connection with the bombings that killed over 200 persons but later he was exonerated by the government and the law enforcement agency. On his release from prison, he married for the second time his long-time girlfriend Rhea Pillai, who had stood by him in his times of grief and travail. She was there by his side when he was being interrogated under TADA for arms possession. Their marriage however did not last long and Rhea and he soon divorced.

The hype surrounding his arrest and his villainous role in the film 'Khalnayak' gave him the much needed career boost and a Filmfare nomination for the Best Actor. Now he has been around twenty-five years in the film industry and he can express agony and despair in a realistic manner due to his tragic life story. He has worked in more than 110 films during these years. Nearly half a dozen films are still on the floor. Although he has done every type of role, he is best suited for rough and tough roles. He has acted in 'Mission Kashmir' as father of Hrithik Roshan. His films, 'Haseena Man Jayegi' and 'Munnabhai MBBS' in 2004 in which he acted as a gangster, a taporia and a doctor have been his most successful films. He won the Filmfare Best Comedian Award for 'Munnabhai MBBS'. He has proved with these films that he is not only an action hero but can do comedy with ease. In 'LoC-Kargil' in the same year his role was more powerful than that of other artistes. In 'Rudraksha' he acted as a tantrik while in 'Sarhad Par' — a film based on Kashmir terrorism, he worked as a truck-driver. In 'Hum Kisise Kam Nahin' with Aishwarya Rai, he acted in an out and out comedy. Mahesh Manjrekar's film 'Rakt' was a flop in 2004. Vidhu Vinod Chopra's film 'Parineeta' with Vidya Balan and based on Sarat Chandra's novel proved a hit with the masses.

'Shabad' was a love story about a writer who is in love with Aishwarya and was an emotional drama. His 'Musafir' in 2000 was shot in Goa but was a flop. It was the story of a don whose money is taken away by his man and to recover which he appoints Anil Kapoor. It was a story of criminals. He also acted in the following films: 'Vande Mataram', 'Nehle pe Dehla', 'Tere Pyar ki Kasam', 'Dus', 'Shaadi No.1', 'Vaah Life ho to Aisi', 'Zinda', etc. He was conferred the Filmfare Award for Best Actor for his acting in the film 'Vaastav' in 2000.

He organised a charity concert for the tsunami victims. Whenever there is a crisis in the country, he comes forward to help the nation. He is doing his bit for AIDS patients too. He has constituted an organisation called the Industry Workers Association for the welfare of the workers and their families. He is very happy in the position he holds today. He gives credit of his success to filmmakers and directors.

* * *

Sanjeev Kumar

Sanjeev Kumar

Harihar Jariwala alias Sanjeev Kumar was a talented actor on both the stage and the silver screen. No matter which role he performed, he did it with utmost dedication. He was a man of principles and established a reputation for performing different roles at the same time. He played the role of a father to Jaya Bhaduri in 'Parichay' in 1972 and subsequently as the lover in 'Anamika' in 1973. He acted as the father to Sharmila Tagore in 'Mausam' and had the unique ability to get into the skin of the role demanded of him. More interestingly he acted as a father-in-law of Jaya Bhaduri in the super hit 'Sholay' in 1975. The renowned filmmaker, Satyajit Ray, made his first Hindi film 'Shatranj ke Khiladi' with Sanjeev Kumar in the lead role.

He belonged to a traditional Gujarati family living in a very small room in Bombay. He was born on 9 July 1937 and was lovingly called Hari Bhai. When he was eighteen-years old, his father died. The entire responsibility of the family fell upon his shoulders. His mother insisted on his taking up a job to run the family, but since his love was the stage since childhood and where he felt he could earn more, he did not think of joining any service.

He was active in Gujarati Theatre. After acting in the theatre, he joined the Filmalaya Acting School where he got the chance to do a small role in the film 'Hum Hindustani' in 1960. He was slated for the lead role in Rajshree Productions' 'Aarti' in 1962 but was dropped in between. While living in a small room of Thakur Sadan, he was cast as an extra in Filmalaya's 'Aao Pyaar Karein' in 1964. Homi Wadia was influenced by his performance and cast him as a hero in his film 'Nishan' in 1965. He struggled for a long time till the film 'Sungharsh' in 1968 with Dilip Kumar became successful. For the first time he established his reputation. He completed K. Asif's incomplete film 'Love and God' after the death of Guru Dutt with all his dedication. He was not only sensitive but also a class performer. His performance as a mentally imbalanced hero in L.V. Prasad's 'Khilona' was superb and commendable. He became a star with this film.

He was a master in enlivening the role, no matter what it was. Rajinder Singh Bedi's 'Dastak' in 1970 became memorable because of his brilliant acting. He won the National Award for Best Actor for this film. His performance in Gulzar's 'Koshish' in 1972 with Jaya Bhaduri as the deaf and dumb wife was outstanding. He won the second National Award for this film.

Sanjeev Kumar became a star after playing successfully different roles in his memorable films like 'Aandhi', 'Mausam', 'Naya Din Nai Raat', 'Parichay', 'Anamika', 'Kitaab', 'Seeta aur Geeta', 'Manchali' and 'Sholay' in 1975. The last named film was a super hit. The role of a revengeful Thakur in 'Sholay' was greatly appreciated. He played nine different roles in 'Naya Din Nai Raat' in 1974. He played the role of a playful husband in 'Pati Patni aur Woh'. 'Trishul' in 1978 was a multi-starrer film and he played his role with utmost restraint. He earned name and fame and won the hearts of the masses. In 'Vidhaata,' in 1982, he played the role of a supporting actor opposite Dilip Kumar and his performance was appreciated. He not only acted serious roles but even comedy too in a manner befitting him. He did challenging roles in 'Meera', 'Naukar', 'Angoor', 'Pati Patni aur Woh', 'Aashirwad', 'Yahi Hai Zindagi', 'Shriman Shrimati' and 'Swarg Narak'. He was known as a serious

and dedicated artiste. The first time he won the Filmfare Award for Best Actor for acting was in 'Aandhi' in 1975 and for the second time for 'Arjun Pandit' in 1976. He had done a good number of films such as 'Raja aur Rank', 'Chanda aur Bijli', 'Anubhav', 'Man Mandir', 'Suraj aur Chanda', 'Manoranjan', 'Silsila', 'Hero' and 'Yaadgaar', etc.

He died an untimely death due to heart failure on 6 November 1985 at the age of forty-eight years. He will always be remembered as a good artiste, versatile actor and a humane gentleman.

* * *

Shabana Azmi

Shabana Azmi is a versatile actress, politician, social activist, promoter of art and culture and has served a term as a nominated member of the Rajya Sabha. She has raised many social and political issues during debates in Parliament.

Born on 18 September 1950 in Delhi, she was given the name Shabana by poet Sardar Zafri. She studied in an English-medium school and graduated from St. Zavier's College. Her father Kaifi Azmi was a socialist and Urdu poet and lyricist. Her mother Shaukat Azmi used to act in plays staged by Prithvi Theatre. Shabana also performed in the play '*Safed Kundali*' and has toured throughout the country and earned name and fame in theatre. Her brother Baba Azmi is also working in the film industry. She married the celebrated poet, lyricist and scriptwriter Javed Akhtar as his second wife.

Her debut film was an art film '*Ankur*' in 1973 and it was directed by renowned director Shyam Benegal and in which she acted as a maidservant. She won the National Film Award for Best Actress for this film in 1974. Although she signed her first film of K.A. Abbas's '*Faasla*', it was released only in 1974. She received the gold medal after training in acting from the Film and Television Institute of India at Pune. She was conferred the Padma Shri in 1998. She has been the goodwill ambassador for the United Nations Population Fund and has participated from time to time in political rallies, hunger strikes and demonstrations for welfare programmes for the downtrodden and the weaker sections of the society.

Shabana has won recognition as an art film actress nationally and internationally. She played the role of a suspicious housewife in '*Shaque*' in 1976. When she switched to acting in commercially successful films like '*Amar Akbar Anthony*' in 1977 after doing serious art films like '*Ankur*' in 1973 and '*Nishant*' in 1975, she was criticized by most of her fans. But after some time, when she displayed her acting ability in both art and commercial cinema, she came to be accepted by one and all. She is a multi-faceted actress and has acted in successful films like '*Avtaar*' with Rajesh Khanna, '*Sparsh*' in 1979, Mahesh Bhatt's '*Arth*' in 1982, Mrinal Sen's '*Khandhar*', Shyam Benegal's '*Mandi*' in 1983 and '*Paar*' in 1985. She became the icon of art and new wave cinema. She has won the National Film Awards for her films '*Arth*', '*Paar*', and '*Khandhar*'.

With the success of her films '*Amar Akbar Anthony*', '*Parvarish*', '*Swami*', '*Junoon*', '*Jwalamukhi*', '*Thodisi Bewafaai*', '*Shart*' and '*Fakira*', she has become a successful star of mainstream cinema too. Her film '*Godmother*' in 1999 won her the National Award for Best Actress. She has worked in international films like John Schlesinger's '*Madame Sousatzka*', '*Immaculate Conception*', Ronald Joffe's '*City of Joy*' and Ismail Merchant's '*In Custody*'. Recently, in 2006, she played a very realistic and touching role in '*15 Park Avenue*' with Waheeda Rehman and Konkona Sen.

* * *

Shammi Kapoor

Shamsher Raj alias 'Yahoo star' Shammi Kapoor was born on 21 October 1931 in Bombay. Simultaneously the first talkie 'Alam Ara' was released in which his father Prithviraj Kapoor played a minor role. Shammi Kapoor was the younger brother of the great showman Raj Kapoor and became known in the film industry as the 'rebel star'. He studied at St. Joseph's Convent, Don Bosco School and New Era School at Bombay. He joined Ruia College and studied science hoping to become an aeronautical engineer. He was an introvert and shy. He left college in between and joined the Prithvi Theatre during adolescence in 1948. He performed roles of child artiste. He acted the role of Bharat in 'Shakuntala'. His tall figure, fair complexion and green eyes made him look like a Greek god. His style of living, dressing and dancing was influenced by Hollywood film-stars. He acted in 'Deewar' in 1945, 'Pathan' in 1947, 'Ghaddar' in 1948, 'Ahooti' in 1949 and 'Kalakar' in 1951. His performances were well acclaimed. He learnt the techniques of theatre and acting. He joined dance classes at the age of seventeen and was inspired by his father to become an actor. His first wife Geeta Bali, whom he married when twenty-eight years of age, on 23 August 1955, was two years senior to him. They were working together in producer-director Hari Walia's film 'Coffee House' at that time. She however died of smallpox on 21 January 1965. He remarried and this time to Neela Devi in 1969 and she is a princess from Bhavnagar. He has a son Aditya and daughter Kanchan (both from Geeta Bali) and a grandson Vishwapratap. A peculiarity of his has been his style of dressing in a loose outfit and not shaving his beard. He shaved last during his ailment in August 2003 when confined to the hospital bed.

His debut film was director Mahesh Kaul's 'Jeevan Jyoti' in 1953 with Chand Usmani as the heroine. He sang a few lines with music director S.D. Burman in this film. He was twenty-one years old. In the same year he acted in 'Gul Sanobar' with Shyama, 'Laila Majnu' with Nutan, 'Rail ka Dibba' with Madhubala and 'Thokar' with Shyama again. These films did little to boost his career. But he continued to do films like 'Chor Bazaar', 'Ehsaan' in 1954, 'Daku', 'Naqab' in 1955, 'Hum Sub Chor Hain', 'Mem Sahib' in 1956 and 'Mirza Sahiban' in 1957, etc. Nasir Husain's musical 'Tumsa Nahin Dekha' in 1957 with debutant heroine Ameeta was a comedy with romance thrown in good measure. It became a great hit and with this film his new image was established. He then performed in 'Dil Deke Dekho' in 1959 with Asha Parekh, in 'Junglee' in 1961 with Saira Banu, 'Professor' in 1962, 'Kashmir ki Kali' and 'Rajkumar' in 1964, 'Teesri Manzil' in 1966 and 'Prince' in 1969. In 'Junglee' while sliding down on the snow-clad mountain, he automatically shouted the word 'yahoo' which became the talk of the town. The song 'Chahe koi mujhe junglee kahe…' of this film became one of the most popular songs. Many songs in this film became hits were primarily due to their music and lyrics. 'Dil Deke Dekho' was a super hit film.

Shammi Kapoor won the Filmfare Award for Best Actor for his role in the film 'Brahmachari' in 1968. Producer F.C. Mehra's film 'Manoranjan' in 1974 was directed by Shammi Kapoor and in which he played an important role with Sanjeev Kumar and Zeenat Aman. Producer Nadiadwala's film 'Bandalbaaz' in 1976 was also directed by him. It was an adaptation of the French play 'Irma La Douce'. His other memorable films were 'Andaaz' in 1971, 'Shalimar' in 1978, 'Meera' in 1979,

'Naseesb' in 1981, 'Prem Rog' in 1982, 'Betaab', 'Hero', 'Sohni Mahival' in 1984, 'Himmat' in 1987, 'Ajooba' in 1991, 'Heer Ranjha' and 'Tahelka' in 1992, 'Prem Granth' in 1998 and 'Censor' in 2001, etc. The Best Supporting Actor's Filmfare Award was conferred upon him for 'Vidhaata' in 1982 while he was given the Filmfare Award for Lifetime Achievements in 1994.

Today Shammi Kapoor leads a retired life and is seen once in a while at film functions.

* * *

Shah Rukh Khan

The king fo celluloid world, Shah Rukh Khan, is today more popular as 'King Khan' or SRK and needs no introduction. He has been one of the biggest heartthrobs of Bollywood in the past one decade. Starting his film journey in 1990, within a span of seventeen years he has performed character roles in about fifty films.

He was born on 2 November 1965 at Talwar Nursing Home in New Delhi to father Mir Taj Muhammed and mother Fatima. The father was a six feet tall Pathan who migrated during the Partition from Pakistan in 1947. He along with his wife settled down in Rajinder Nagar, New Delhi, to run a furniture and transport business He, however, died of cancer in 1981. Shah Rukh's mother Fatima hailed from Hyderabad and was a social worker as were as officer. She is no longer alive.

Shah Rukh Khan has an older sister Shenaz who is six years older than him. He studied in St. Columba's School where he was awarded the 'sword of honour' for being chosen the best student in school. He used to do small roles in school and also imitate his teachers. He then joined Hans Raj College and graduated in economics with first division (1985-88) before joining the Jamia Milia Islamia for doing Masters in mass communication. Since his younger days he had an innate passion for making advertising films. He did small roles in stage shows at Kamani Auditorium and earned many awards.

In 1984, he met Gauri Chhiba, daughter of a retired Major Ramesh Chhiba from a Hindu Brahmin family, but he could marry her only in 1991 as he had to face initial resistance to the marriage by Gauri's parents. He now has two children, son Aryan and daughter Suhana. Despite acting with the most beautiful actresses, Shah Rukh has never been linked romantically to any of them. He is basically a family man and spends his free time with his children, whenever he can. He lives in a sea-facing bungalow named 'Mannat' where both Lord Ganesha and Prophet Mohammed are worshipped.

Shah Rukh began his carrer on TV with a serial entitled '*Fauji*' which won him instant recognition. He also acted in other TV soaps '*Circus*' and '*Dil Dariya*', before taking the leap into feature films with '*Deewana*' in which Rishi Kapoor and Divya Bharti acted in stellar roles in 1993. This film became the first film of his in a string of blockbusters to follow and established him as India's most bankable star. Producer G.P. Sippy gave him the chance to show his talent in his film '*Rajoo Ban Gaya Gentleman*' in a role moulded in Raj Kapoor style. During the same period, on seeing his enthusiasm, Hema Malini, the famous Dream Girl of Hindi cinema, cast him as the hero in her maiden directorial debut film '*Dil Ashna Hai*'. This was preceded by another multi-starrer film '*Chamatkar*' by Eagle Films.

Without any godfather in the film industry of Bollywood but blessed with a powerful screen presence and ability to accept any role that was given to him Shah Rukh Khan continued to explore his goal with grit and determination. He stunned his audiences by doing anti-hero roles and that too in a row of three films '*Bazigar*', '*Darr*' and '*Anjaam*'. Such was his characterisation of the roles that he was conferred with the Best Villain Award for the film '*Anjaam*'. It is worthy note that no hero

in his early film career would have accepted to take the risk of acting in such an anti-hero role and get typed in the image of the villain. But SRK accepted the challenge successfully. The masses accepted his films that went on to become box-office hits.

In 1994, he proved himself a good actor by acting in hit film 'Kabhi Khushi Kabhi Gham' and his super-duper action thriller 'Karan Arjun' was well received by the audiences all over the country. Since then there was no looking back. He has won several awards for his outstanding performances in 1995 in 'Dilwale Dulhaniya Le Jayenge', 'Dil to Pagal Hai' in 1997, 'Kuch Kuch Hota Hai' in 1998 and 'Badshah' in 1999. These were followed by Subhash Ghai's 'Pardesh', Mani Ratnam's 'Dil Se' and Aditya Chopra's 'Mohabbatein' which cemented his image not only in India but abroad too, where he has proven a good foreign exchange earner.

Shah Rukh very ably portrayed the role of a romantic hero when he performed love scenes with his teacher in 'Main Hoon Na'. During the shooting of this film, he suffered from an intense backache, but he completed the film by taking painkillers. The film was successful at the box-office. Subsequently he was rushed to London for a successful but delicate operation of his back which, if a failure, could have rendered him immobile for the rest of his life.

Shah Rukh's film 'Swadesh' did not earn much financial benefits for the director and producer but it got rave reviews in the press and by discerning viewers, both within and abroad. He won the Filmfare Power Award and Best Actor Award for 2004. Director Yash Chopra's film 'Veer Zara' revealed him as a most talented and serious artiste. This film won many awards in the country.

Shah Rukh then began branching out into other fields and launched his own production company by the name of Dreamz Unlimited in partnership with his co-star Juhi Chawla to produce 'Phir Bhi Dil Hai Hindustani'. While this labour of love did not go down well with the audiences, it apparently served a good opening in the international market, where SRK has a loyal following among the non-resident Indians. He even produced a period film 'Asoka' in 2001 and rendered a few songs in some of his films like 'Josh', 'Hum Hain Lajawaab', etc. His ambitious film 'Paheli' opposite Rani Mukherjee was nominated for the Oscar Award. It was one of the greatest honours for him. His 'Devdas' was shown in the Cannes Film Festival under the non-competitive section.

One characteristic of Shah Rukh's personality, which no one can hope to match, is his boundless energy. Even if the public is his worst critic and whether he is taking you through a mindless comedy like 'Duplicate' or an intense romance like 'Dil Se', his passion and energy are infectious. These are some qualities that you cannot ignore easily and these are perhaps, the essence of his charisma. There is no disputing the fact that Shah Rukh Khan is the most saleable Bollywood star today among the youngsters in India.

Shah Rukh Khan organises and performs in high energy stage shows in India and abroad. He was conferred the Zee Cine Award in London in 2005 and Best Actor Award for 'Veer Zara'. He models for a number of consumer products, both for Indian and international corporate

houses. He is friendly by nature and endowed with a funny sense of humour. He has a number of major film projects in hand by renowned filmmakers and these are yet to be released.

Such is Shah Rukh's stature today that neither success nor failure of any particular film is likely to shake the people's faith in him or cause a dent in his reputation. King Khan is here for a long and glorious innings that has only just begun.

* * *

Shashi Kapoor

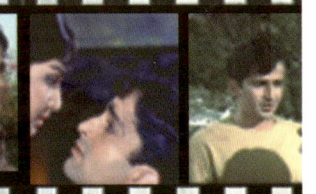

Shashi Kapoor

Shashi Kapoor, the youngest son of veteran and legendary celebrity Prithviraj Kapoor, was born on 18 March 1938. When his father shifted to Bombay, he studied at Don Bosco School. His father used to call him 'Shashilala' because, being the youngest, he loved him very much. During his childhood days, Prithvi Theatres came into being on 15 January 1944. Their first play 'Shakuntala' was staged on 9 March 1945 at the Royal Opera House. Shashi for the first time acted as part of a crowd scene at the age of six only. Subsequently, 'Deewar' was staged on 9 August 1947 and he played the role of a little son. Another play 'Pathan' was staged on 13 April 1947 and Shashi played the role of Bahadur Khan, son of a nationalist Muslim. When he grew older, he was made an assistant stage manager of Prithvi Theatres and entrusted the responsibility to introduce new techniques in the art of theatre. His passion continues to be the theatre still.

His elder brother Raj Kapoor directed and produced his first film 'Aag' in 1948 wherein Shashi enacted the childhood role of Raj Kapoor for fifteen minutes at the age of nine. He also played a child's role in 'Samadhi' in 1950. In the film 'Awara' in 1951, he was acclaimed internationally for his role as a child.

While Prithviraj was shooting the climax of K. Asif's historical film 'Mughal-e-Azam' at Jaipur, Shashi got married at the age of twenty years to Jennifer Kendal. She was an English girl who was daughter of Geoffrey Kendal, who ran his own theatre company called Shakespeareana. Shashi joined this company in February 1957 to learn the new techniques of theatre acting. His clear pronunciation in English was admired by the Kendal family. He toured many cities and staged Shakespeare's plays with this company. He rejoined Prithvi Theatres in 1958.

After marriage, his son Kunal was born and Shashi decided to join films. His debut film, 'Char Diwari' in 1961 starring Nanda was an art film. It did not get him any credit. Producer B.R. Chopra's 'Dharamputra' in 1961 based on a very sensitive issue was well appreciated but he did not get much credit for it. James Ivory and Ismail Merchant produced an English film 'Householder' in 1963, with him as the hero but this film could not be digested by the Indian masses. The Hindi commercial cinema did not accept him as he was called the 'English' Kapoor. His lead role in the English film 'Shakespeare' in 1965 was appreciated at the International Film Festival. His American film 'Pretty Polly' in 1968 was acclaimed. He continued with his efforts in films like 'Prem Patra' in 1962, 'Yeh Dil Kisko Doon' in 1963, 'Benazir' in 1964, but none of them established him as a successful actor. His luck clicked with 'Jab Jab Phool Khile' in 1965 opposite Nanda. The film was shot in the colourful land of Kashmir and was provided with melodious songs and music. The film was well accepted by the public.

In the same year, B.R. Films released 'Waqt', a multi-starrer on a big budget. It became a super hit and he became a much sought after star. Films like 'Pyaar Kiye Ja' and 'Aamne Samne' were average films. His successful films were 'Hasina Maan Jayegi' in 1968, 'Ek Shriman Ek Shrimati' in 1969, 'Sharmilee' in 1971, 'Aa Gale Lag Ja' in 1973 and 'Roti Kapada aur Makan' in 1974. These films established him as a successful star of Bollywood. He acted in the controversial film 'Siddharth' too.

A turning point in his film career came with director Yash Chopra's film 'Deewar' in 1975 in which he acted with Amitabh Bachchan. It was a film of two brothers, one on the side of law and the other, a criminal. It was a super hit film. His pariring with Amitabh Bachchan in films like 'Kabhi Kabhi', 'Trishul', 'Suhaag', 'Kala Patthar' and 'Silsila' won him accolades. He won the Filmfare Award for Best Supporting Actor in 'Deewar'. In the Indio-Soviet production 'Ajooba' in 1991, he directed Amitabh Bachchan and his elder brother Shammi Kapoor but it was an average film. He produced a few films — 'Junoon', 'Kalyug', '36 Chowringhee Lane', 'Vijeta' in 1983 and 'Utsav' in 1985 the last named caused him heavy financial losses. His performance in 'Junoon' and director Girish Karnad's 'Utsav' opposite Rekha were critically acclaimed. Subsequently his lively performance in Raj Kapoor's 'Satyam Shivam Sundaram' in 1978 with the glamorous Zeenat Aman can never be forgotten. His other memorable films were 'Kranti', 'Namak Halal', 'New Delhi Times' in 1985 and 'Muhafiz' in 1993. He was conferred the National Award for Best Actor for 'New Delhi Times'. He worked in 'Heat and Dust' in 1973, 'Samy and Rosy' in 1987, then in 'The Deceivers' and in Ismail Merchant's 'In Custody'.

He decided to retire from the film world in 1992. He now leads a contented and retired life by keeping busy with various social activities. According to him, There is no magic formula to instant stardom; the road to the top is steep and determination, perseverance and sweat can take you there. He and his family members along with other well-wishers are determined to keep the flag of Prithvi Theatres flying.

* * *

Sunny Deol

The rough and tough macho star Sunny Deol alias Ajay Singh Deol was born on 19 October 1956 in New Delhi. He is five feet nine inches tall and has a well-developed body. His Punjabi Jat father, Dharmendra, is a renowned film star and elected Member of Parliament from Bikaner. His mother Prakash Kaur is a housewife. His brother Bobby Deol and step-sister Esha Deol have also established themselves successfully in Bollywood. He is married to Pooja and has two children.

He won the Filmfare Award for '*Ghayal*' in 1990 and the National Award for Best Supporting Actor in '*Damini*' in 1993. According to him, he did not want to be an actor but was keen to become an electronic engineer. He however used to accompany his father during the school holidays on shootings and developed the desire to become an actor during the first year of his college. He enjoyed his stay in London where he led an independent life and joined the British Theatre Company for a year to perform in plays. On retuning to Bombay, he joined Roshan Taneja's School of Acting and that is when he decided to join films. His main problem was that he was very shy and an introvert.

His debut film was director Rahul Rawail's '*Betaab*' in 1983 with debutant heroine Amrita Singh. It was an action film and clicked at the box-office. In this first film, he proved his star talent. He became an action hero and it helped him in improving his confidence. Subsequently in 1984, he acted in director Raj Khosla's '*Sunny*', producer F.C. Mehra's '*Sohni Mahiwal*' and Nasir Husain's '*Manzil Manzil*' with Dimple Kapadia. While working in these films, he learnt the tricks of the trade and many new things. He became very close to Dimple too.

He was cast again by Nasir Husain in '*Zabardast*' and by Rahul Rawail in '*Arjun*' in 1985. His performance and excellent chemistry with Dimple Kapadia was well appreciated and '*Arjun*' became a successful film at the box-office. In '*Dacait*' in 1987, he acted as a peace-loving guy who becomes a dacoit to seek revenge against the Thakur who kills his brother and sister. The film did not do well at the box-office. He played the role of an orphan in '*Yateem*' and director Rajiv Rai's '*Tridev*' became a commercially successful film. Director Raj Kumar Santhoshi's '*Ghayal*' was the story of a boxer and was produced by Dharmendra; it became a huge hit and won the Filmfare Award. In '*Damini*' in 1990, he performed the character role of a drunken lawyer and won the National Award. A dialogue '*Yeh dhai kilo ka haath jis per pad gaya toh…*' of this film became popular. With the box-office success of '*Tridev*', '*Ghayal*', '*Darr*', '*Damini*', '*Jeet*', '*Lootere*' and '*Chalbaaz*' he proved himself to be a successful actor. He acted as a simple village boy in '*Ghatak*' in 1996 and in the film '*Jeet*' in 1996 with Salman Khan, proving that he could act varied roles. Director-producer J.P. Dutta's '*Border*' in 1997 was a war film based on the battle of Longewala that took place in 1971 and the film did well and his role was appreciated.

Sunny became a director-producer with his film '*Dillagi*' in 1999 and it was critically well appreciated. The film '*Gadar, Ek Prem Katha*' in 2001 with Amisha Patel was again a love story between a rich princess and a poor truck-driver with the Partition as the backdrop. It became the biggest blockbuster of all time. A film on the renowned freedom fighter Bhagat Singh, and titled

'23rd march-1931 Shaheed' in 2002, was produced by him and he played the character of Chandrashekhar Azad while his brother Bobby Deol acted the role of Shaheed Bhagat Singh. He played the role of an ex-student of a college in 'Rok Sako to Rok Lo' in 2004. In his home production 'Socha na Tha' he introduced his cousin Abhay Deol and it proved an average film. His brilliant performance in 'Jo Bole so Nihaal' in 2005 was liked but the film faced protests from a section of the society. His film 'Teesri Aankh' in 2006 with Amisha Patel was based on sex crime and he acted as a dignified police officer.

Sunny carries essentially the image of an action hero. He has performed all types of roles and wants to do one or two films at a time. He is in perennial demand with filmmakers. He has some good films yet to be released. His some other memorable films are 'Samundar', 'Joshilaa', 'Gunaah', 'Kshatriya', 'Angrakshak', 'Salaakhein', 'Arjun Pandit', 'Champion', 'Khel' and 'Leader, Forbidden Lines' in 2004. During the shooting of the film 'Dacait', he fell down from his horse and injured his back. He underwent a successful operation and is well and fit for his next shoot.

* * *

Sunil Dutt

Sunil Dutt

Sunil Dutt was a renowned politician, respected actor, producer, director, secularist, philanthropist, social activist, a kind human being and lastly, Union Minister of Youth Affairs and Sports before he breathed his last on 25 May 2005 in Mumbai in his sleep. He is survived by his only son, Sanjay Dutt and two daughters, Namrata and Priya. He was seventy-five-years old.

Born in 1930 in a Kurd village of Jhelum district, now in Pakistan, he lost his father at the age of five. He was a student of Mumbai's Jai Hind College. He began as a radio-show host and celebrity interviewer, which led to his entry into the film world. He was a successful politician and won the General Elections to the Lok Sabha five times but it was only at the age of seventy-four, i.e. in the year 2004, that he was for the first time appointed as the Union Minister in the Central Government. He won the first Lok Sabha election in 1984. He was appointed *Sadbhavana ka Sipahi* in 2002.

After his death, his ashes were immersed in River Ganges by his son Sanjay Dutt. His daughters Namrata and Priyanka, brothers-in-law Kumar Gaurav and Owen Roncen and three nieces were present at his death-bed.

Sunil Dutt's real name was Balraj Dutt and nickname was Balloo but filmmaker Ramesh Saigal changed his name to Sunil Dutt in his debut film *'Railway Platform'* in which he acted with actress Nalini Jaywant in 1955. He had great love and affection for his village. He shot his entire film *'Dakoo aur Jawan'* in this village. He was lovingly called Papaji by the villagers. He was a staunch promoter of secularism. He built a senior secondary school that housed about 1,600 students and it was accessible through a smooth road from the village to the highway. He was a great lover of Urdu poetry and had built a *samadhi* in memory of his mother near the banks of River Yamuna where his mother was cremated.

'Ek hi Rasta' in 1956 marked the start of a seven-film long association with B.R. Chopra. Dutt's true breakthrough however came with Mehboob Khan's magnum opus *'Mother India'* in 1957. His portrayal of Birju, Nargis's rebellious younger son, portrayed a new and energetic actor. Dutt's association with Nargis in the movie resulted in his marrying her after the release of the film.

Dutt's role in women-oriented films like *'Sadhna'* in 1958, *'Sujata'* in 1959 and *'Main Chup Rahungi'* in 1962 were well appreciated and noted filmmakers like Bimal Roy and Hrishikesh Mukherjee began to cast him in their films.

Sunil Dutt was a down-to-earth family man who cared not only for his own family but for the families of all those who were close to him. Once he said about his son Sanjay, He is making money but I am earning love. His money will get spent, but the respect and love that I get will remain for him when I leave. I only hope he keeps it up. Somewhere, I am sure he will take care of my respect and love.

During his *padyatra* from Mumbai to the Golden Temple in Amritsar in 1987 with daughter Priya, a Christian boy from Kerala accompanied the *padyatris*. A foreign journalist asked the boy what he

felt about the *padyatra*. He replied thus: "I have heard about Christ but I am very happy that I am walking with Christ," obviously referring to Sunil Dutt.

Sunil Dutt was a fighter and continued to struggle all his life. He had seen many ups and downs in his life. He was a successful actor, producer and director. In 1962, he formed the Ajanta Arts and went to the border to entertain the Jawans. As a producer he experimented boldly by directing his one-hero first film *'Yaadein'* in 1964, which won the National Film Award — a certificate of merit. He lost a lot of money when the public did not appreciate the film. His next directorial venture *'Reshma aur Shera'* in 1971 showed his artistic impulses.

He worked in *'Kundan'*, *'Rajdhani'*, *'Kismat ka Khel'*, *'Ek hi Rasta'* and *'Payal'* too. He acted in about 102 films during the five decades of his acting career. He not only acted a lead hero but also as an anti-hero successfully in films *'Mujhe Jeene Do'*, *'Reshma aur Shera'* and *'Pran Jaye par Vachan na Jaye'*. He acted as a fugitive in *'36 Ghante'* and a cold-blooded assassin and jealous husband who kills his wife's lover in *'Yeh Raaste Hain Pyar Ke'* in 1963. He dared to play a cripple in *'Khandaan'*. He showed his brilliant performances in *'Sujata'*, *'Amrapali'*, *'Mera Saaya'*, *'Gumraah'*. In the last-named film he was the first actor who played the *'other man'* in an extra-marital love story. He worked in *'Waqt'*, *'Hamraaz'*, *'Nagin'*, *'Raj Tilak'*, *'Jaani Dushman'* and the hilarious film *'Padosan'*. He also won the Filmfare Award for Best Actor in 1963 for *'Mujhe Jeene Do'* and in 1965 for *'Khandaan'*.

He was honoured with the responsibility of being appointed the Sherrif for some time in Mumbai. He also acted and directed as an anguished father watching his daughter die in *'Dard ka Rishta'* and *'Yeh Aag Kab Bujhegi'* in 1982. He also produced the film *'Rocky'* to launch his son Sanjay in 1981 but this film was released after the death of Nargis. After her untimely death in 1981 due to cancer, he successfully entered into the politics in 1984. In memory of his wife he established the Nargis Dutt Memorial Foundation in 1981. In 1993 his life once again took a turn for the worse when his son Sanjay was arrested under TADA for illegal possession of arms.

His other memorable films are *'Usne Kaha Tha'*, *'Ghazal'*, *'Milan'*, *'Heera'*, *'Geeta Mera Naam'*, *'Virodhi'*, *'Parampara'*, *'Phool'*, *'Kshatriya'* and his last film with son Sanjay was *'Munna Bhai MBBS'* in which he worked as father to Sanjay.

He was also associated with the Cancer Patients Aid Association, National Association for the Blind and the Spastics Society of India. In his last letter he donated one lakh rupees to the widow of a migrant labourer from Uttar Pradesh who had donated his organs to save six other lives. As his last wish he desired, "There should be no statues or a street named after me, no postal stamp with my face or any organisation after me. I'd like people to remember me by following my work."

* * *

    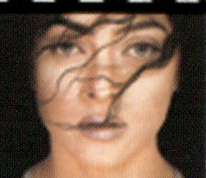

Sushmita Sen

This is the girl who became Miss Universe at the young age of eighteen when girls are in school or planning to join college. She was posed the question, "What is the essence of a woman?" in the international beauty pageant and she replied, "Just being a woman is God's gift. The origin of a child is a mother, a woman. She shows a man what sharing, caring and loving is all about. That is the essence of a woman." These lines were met with a thunderous applause before she was announced Miss Universe 1994. She was so shocked to hear the jury's verdict that all she could do was to gape at them, her hands covering her mouth in disbelief and tears trickling down her cheeks. She had indeed placed her country on the world map.

Sushmita's father comes from Defence Services and this meant having to travel from one state to another and leading a nomadic life. Finally as she grew older, her mother decided to shift base to Delhi to bring a semblance of permanency in her children's lives and impart them proper education. So Sushmita was put in an English-medium school that she found tough to cope with but her parents insisted on her studying there as they knew her potential.

In school itself, Sushmita showed not only brains, but oozed confidence and self-control. Being five feet eleven inches tall and adequately good-looking, she decided to participate in beauty pageants held in India and also do modelling. She first made her entry into the fashion world and took part in a few fashion shows before participating in the Femina Miss India pageant. Here the competition was tough as beauties from all over country participated. In the contest she went on to win the Femina Miss India crown, defeating her arch rival and more popular, the light-eyed Aishwarya Rai. She then followed this up by winning the Miss Universe tiara. Her poise and grace came to her help and as the press said that it was "a little of everything…the height…the spirit that lights her up which compensated for her lack of classical beauty."

With the crown came the responsibility of representing the country wherever she went, but with her charming personality she won accolades all over. No sooner did her term as Miss Universe got over that she decided to try her hand at acting in films. Producer Mukesh Bhatt's '*Dastak*' in 1996 was her debut film and she played the role of a vulnerable girl who is stalked by a psycho man. The script of this film was written keeping her in mind. But this film did not get her recognition in Bollywood. Thereafter she performed in some other films like '*Ratchakra*' and '*Zor*' in 1997 and the Telugu film '*Mudhalvan*' in 1999 but none of these films influenced the masses. She was dubbed too Westernised, too tall for Indian heroes. Though her films did not do well, her performances were well appreciated by the critics. Her sizzling dance number on the song '*Dilber, dilber…*' in '*Sirf Tum*' was acclaimed by the masses. Then came '*Biwi Number One*' in 1999 in which she caught the media's attention. She effectively played the role of the second wife with Karishma Kapoor. Her guest appearance in '*Fiza*' in 2000 and her sexy item song '*Mehboob mere mehboob…*' was amply talked about by the audience. She gave an impressive performance in Meghna Gulzar's '*Filhaal*' in 2002 with a convincing portrayal of her character in the film. She then played a classic role of a helpless woman before Amitabh Bachchan, who abducts her brother in '*Aankhe*'. She brilliantly

performed the role of an Assistant Commissioner of Police in 'Samay' in 2003, acting with all seriousness and soon becoming the choice of filmmakers.

Some of her films like 'Hindustan ki Kasam', 'Aaghaz', 'Bas Itna sa Khwaab Hai', 'Kyon ki Main Jhooth Nahin Bolta', 'Tum ko na Bhool Paayenge' and 'Leela' were average or below average. Her role in the film 'Main Hoon Na' as a modern teacher proved her to be a talented actress. She worked with Salman Khan in 'Maine Pyaar Kyon Kiya' in 2005, 'Mai Aisa Hi Hoon', 'Kisna', 'Bewafaa' and 'Vastu Shastra' established her as a successful heroine of Bollywood. She played a memorable role of a Bengali prostitute in director Kalpana Lajmi's film 'Chingaari' in 2006 with actor Mithun Chakravaorty. The film was not successful at the box-office but her performance was appreciated. Some of her major and important films are yet to come. She has always done the kind of films and roles that she believes in. She lives and works on her own terms.

Sushmita has strong maternal feelings and soon after winning the Miss Universe title adopted a girl-child and named her Renee. She gives full attention to her needs and independent development. She is happy with the child.

* * *

Vyjyanthimala

Bharatanatyam exponent Vyjayanthimala hails from Madras and was born in 1936. Her debut film in Tamil-Telugu languages was 'Life'; subsequently she acted in another Tamil film 'Vijaya Kumari'. The name of her Tamil film was 'Vazhkai' and in Telugu, it was 'Jeevitham'. She has been the first actress to join Bollywood from the south. Producer AVM's Hindi film 'Bahar' in 1951 with Karan Dewan was her debut film. They produced another film 'Ladki' in 1953 in Tamil and Telugu languages but its Hindi version had hero Bharat Bhushan, keeping in view that a larger number of cine-goers would see the film in Hindi. In between, 'Anjaan' with Prem Nath as the hero was released in 1952. The film 'Bahar' marked her presence in Bollywood, but did little to boost her career. In 1954, she performed in 'Miss Mala', 'Pehali Jhalak' with Kishore Kumar and in Filmistan's 'Nagin' with Pradeep Kumar. She became a hit star with the super success of 'Nagin' in 1954 which was directed by Nandlal Jaswantlal and contained melodious as well as lilting music composed by renowned musician, Hemant Kumar. The film repeatedly drew crowds for months. She performed a bewitching snake dance on the song 'Mann dole mera tan dole…' and 'Jadoogar saiyan…' which became very popular throughout the country.

Director-producer Bimal Roy, influenced by her star performance, cast her as a prostitute in his film 'Devdas' in 1955 opposite Dilip Kumar. She proved true to the aspirations of Bimal Roy and the film was well acclaimed by the critics and the public. It became a hit film. As she was a dancer, she could perform long dance sequences whenever demanded by the script. She set the trend for the future incoming heroines and conveyed that being a dancer added to one's acting ability. She rose to stardom with the success of 'Naya Daur' in 1957, 'Madhumati' in 1958, 'Ganga Jamuna' in 1961 — all with Dilip Kumar and 'Sadhna' in 1958 with Sunil Dutt. Her performance in RK Films 'Sangam' in 1964 with Raj Kapoor and Rajinder Kumar became the most memorable film of her career. This film's song 'Main kya karoon Ram mujhe budha mil gaya…' created a wave among the music lovers. She became a money-earner and much sought after heroine of Bollywood. She won the Filmfare Best Actress Awards for 'Sadhna', 'Ganga Jamuna' and 'Sangam'. Director Vijay Anand's 'Jewel Thief' in 1967 with Dev Anand as the hero was a suspense drama and proved a successful film. She was drawn towards the already married Raj Kapoor for some time but she finally married Raj Kapoor's personal physician, Dr Bali. She had to wait for him to get divorce from his first wife. She left the film industry in despair. She had a son with Dr Bali and decided to devote herself to various business activities.

Vyjayanthimala turned to politics and became a Member of Parliament from Madras after leaving films. She was conferred the Lifetime Achievement Award of Filmfare in 1995. Though she has left films, her interest in dance continues. Her other memorable films are 'New Delhi', 'Amardeep', 'Raj Tilak', 'Paigham', 'Jhoola', 'Leader', 'Amrapali', 'Prince' and 'Pyaar hi Pyaar'. She played successfully in Bangla film 'Hate Bazaare Too' She now leads a retired life.

* * *

Waheeda Rehman

Waheeda Rehman

Waheeda Rehman, a versatile south Indian classical dancer in Telugu films, was born on 3 February 1938 in Hyderabad. She studied only up to matriculation She was introduced to Bollywood by the talented actor-director-producer Guru Dutt. He cast her as a vamp in his film 'CID' in 1956 and it was a crime-thriller starring Dev Anand, Shakila and Johnny Walker. The film was successful at the box-office all over India due to its music, songs and picturisation. In Telugu her debut film was 'Jayasimha' in 1955.

Her next film 'Pyaasa' in 1957 was the first directorial masterpiece of Guru Dutt. It was the story of a poet struggling to find recognition in the materialistic world. She acted as the sympathetic prostitute Gulabo who gets his poems published without his knowledge and earns name and fame for him. The film reflected the relations between a writer and a selfish publisher. It was a hit film because of its direction, music, popular songs and her graceful performance. With the box-office hit of these two films, she became a popular star. By this time she and Guru Dutt came very close to each other. It is said that the song 'Aaj sajan mohe ang laga lo…' of 'Pyaasa' brought them together.

Waheeda worked as an accomplished star in Guru Dutt's 'Kaagaz ke Phool' in 1959 which was a biographical film. It was shot beautifully and artistically on the life of a successful filmmaker. This classic proved an utter failure at the box-office but it later became a landmark in Indian cinema. She reached the highest pinnacle in the industry and started acting in films made by other directors too. Meanwhile her mentor Guru Dutt's married status came in the way. Their relations became strained. However, she performed seriously and with all dedication her role in 'Sahib Biwi aur Ghulam' in 1962. It was s super hit at the box-office. She became a hot star of the day. Her other film 'Bees Saal Baad' in 1962 with Biswajit in the lead was a suspense thriller with catchy songs and melodious music. Now there was no stopping her. She was on the top run of the ladder in acting.

In director Vijay Anand's masterpiece film 'Guide' made in 1965, she intelligently and realistically performed the role of wife Rosie. Her enchanting acting on the song 'Aaj phir jeene ki tamanna hai…' with Dev Anand became a major attraction of the film. The film is the story of an unhappy wife who initially loves the guide Raju but later on gets antagonised against him due to various reasons. The film was successful. She did 'Kohra', 'Majboor', 'Shagun', 'Dil Diya Dard Liya', 'Aadmi', 'Ram aur Shyam', 'Neelkamal', all of which were average films. Her remarkable performances in 'Teesri Kasam' in 1966, 'Palki' in 1967, 'Khamoshi' in 1969, 'Mujhe Jeene Do', 'Prem Pujari' in 1970, 'Reshma aur Shera' in 1971, 'Chaudhvin ka Chaand' and 'Dil Ek Mandir' in 1972 are worth mentioning as these helped to strengthen her position in Bollywood.

Waheeda shocked the film-folk by marrying her one-time co-star and businessman Kamaljeet in 1974 to settle down in Bangalore. She temporarily retired from films. At times she appeared in character roles of her choice in films and TV serials.

She started playing character roles after some years of marriage in films like 'Kabhi-Kabhi' in 1976

and 'Trishul'. Her roles as an elderly woman in 'Naseeb' in 1982, 'Chandni' in 1989, 'Lamhe' in 1991 and 'Om Jai Jagdish' in 2002 were well acclaimed.

Her husband is no longer alive and she is leading a contented life with her son and daughter. She won the Filmfare Awards for 'Guide' and 'Neel Kamal' and was honoured with the Filmfare Lifetime Achievement Award in 1994.

* * *

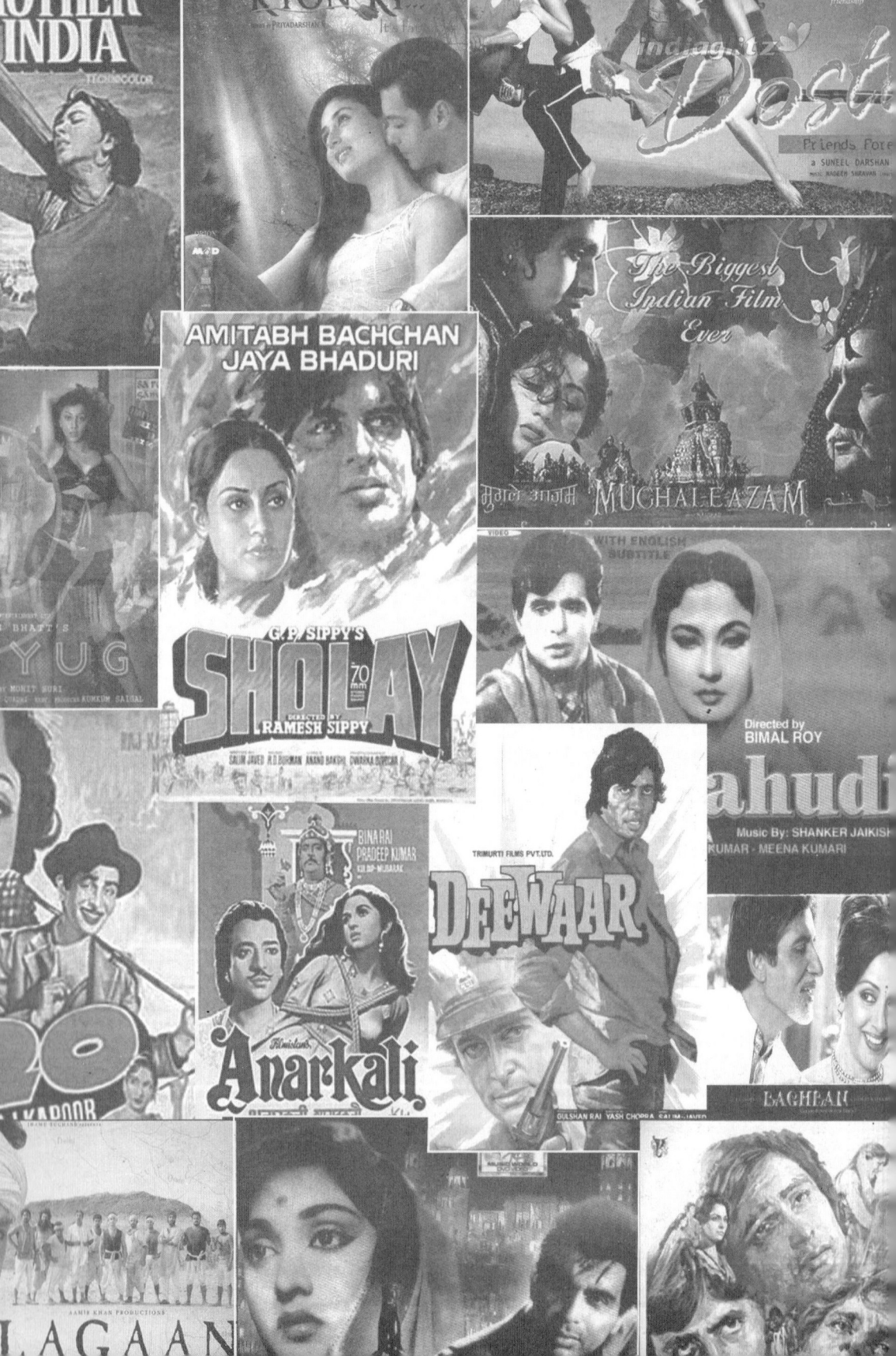